W9-BCW-756

THE POPULIST RESPONSE
TO INDUSTRIAL AMERICA

329.8
P

THE POPULIST RESPONSE
TO INDUSTRIAL AMERICA

Midwestern Populist Thought

NORMAN POLLACK

✤

HARVARD UNIVERSITY PRESS
CAMBRIDGE, MASSACHUSETTS · 1962

WINGATE COLLEGE LIBRARY
WINGATE, N. C.

© Copyright, 1962, by the President and Fellows
of Harvard College

All rights reserved

Distributed in Great Britain by Oxford University Press, London

Publication of this book has been aided by a grant
from the Ford Foundation

Library of Congress Catalog Card Number: 62-20249

Printed in the United States of America

TO MY
MOTHER

AND TO THE MEMORY OF MY
FATHER
BENJAMIN POLLACK

WHO WORKED HIMSELF
TO DEATH IN A VAIN SEARCH
FOR THE AMERICAN DREAM

22202

CONTENTS

THE POPULIST RESPONSE
TO INDUSTRIAL AMERICA

———————— ✛ ————————

INTRODUCTION

The industrial transformation in the United States has not been viewed with the bold penetration found in studies of European capitalist development. There is still no American Mosca, Pirenne, Weber, or Marx to discuss the alignment of social forces during the emergence of industrial society. This failure to enlarge our horizons is totally unnecessary; a body of excellent monographs already exists for placing industrialism in a wider perspective. Yet, despite the existence of these studies, historians have not asked truly significant questions of their data. The result is a continuous accumulation of facts which directly contradict prevailing notions on industrialism. The foundation for a synthesis is present, but we seem farther away than ever from reconciling fact and theory. This book, by focusing on the agrarian response, is intended as a tentative first step toward the more comprehensive analysis of industrial America. The role of agrarianism is a fitting point of departure. In the transition to industrialism this group uniquely reveals the potential sources for conflict in the society, the social costs involved in the emergence of a new economy, and, because agrarians remain at the periphery of these changes, the possibility of a detached and searching critique unknown to those caught up by the system. Here agrarianism serves as the conscience of the social order and its chief protagonist.

To view the anatomy of industrial America from this perspective, one must begin with these questions: Did Populism accept industrialism and social change, basing its protest on what it believed to be the realities of the 1890's? Or did it seek instead to restore pre-industrial society, comprehending neither the major trends of its age nor the solutions necessary to cope with these altered circumstances? Was Populism therefore a progressive or retrogressive, a forward- or backward-looking, social force? The disparity noted above is nowhere better seen than in the conclusion reached by historians on these questions. Whatever their personal view of the movement, itself important because Populism has had its critics as well as supporters, and whatever their field of specialization, historians agree in regarding it, in the words of Professor John D. Hicks, as "beginning the last phase of a long and perhaps losing struggle—the struggle to save agricultural America from the devouring jaws of industrial America." [1]

That this retrogressive framework can be supported through the examples of numerous industrial revolutions is undeniable; clearly, agrarians often aligned with conservative groups in the vain attempt to turn back history. Nor do the results appear different when agrarian movements acted alone and in a radical direction, for they seemed generally incapable of combining with industrial labor to promote a society both democratic *and* industrial. Thus, whether radical or conservative, agrarianism in a world perspective takes on the shape of a retrogressive social force. It would, however, be a serious mistake merely to assume that all industrial transformations follow the same pattern. I submit that while the generalization is not without foundation, the American experience proves a notable exception. For three reasons, this difference has not been sufficiently appreciated: The belief that agrarianism must act retrogressively, deduced usually from situations of abrupt transition from feudalism to capitalism, is no longer questioned; Americanists have followed suit, accepting this view and then confining their research to more specific problems; and most important, the actual evidence on the agrarian response to industrialism has not hitherto been presented.

Yet, the overwhelming evidence of previous scholarship flatly contradicts the retrogressive framework on three notable grounds—the relation of agrarians to technology, politics, and industrial labor. On the first, accounts of post-Civil War agricultural practices are at one in demonstrating that farmers, far from opposing technology, were receptive to mechanization, scientific procedures, and the dissemination of technical information. Solon J. Buck's standard work on the Granger movement, discussing its educative function along these lines, is one case in point. Moreover, as Buck further shows, this attitude was translated into political activity. Confronting specific transportation abuses, Grangers did not seek to abolish railroads but rather "to subject them to public control." Grangerism, then, does not comport with the image of agrarians as resisting social change; one does not find here the Luddite response to technology.[2]

Looking more directly at the political solutions of

Populism, scholars agree that the movement offered highly concrete remedies designed to meet *existing* conditions, a stand quite different from what one would expect of a backward-looking movement. Populism did not propose utopian blueprints for the perfect society of independent yeomanry. Its measures, while predicated on the opposition to monopoly, were not bent upon eradicating the very principle of bigness. When Hicks notes, within the retrogressive framework, that Populists "catalogued in their platform the evils from which society suffered and suggested the specific remedies by which these evils were to be overcome," he provides a classic illustration of this paradox in historical interpretation: copious documentation of a progressive movement placed in the context of a declining social force.[3]

But the framework does not necessarily assume an inconspicuous role. It exerts a decisive influence in areas where further research might call into question its very validity. This is illustrated by the way historians approach the problem of a farmer-labor coalition. Reasoning that agrarians desire a world without factories—and without industrial workers—historians conclude *in advance* that Populist views on labor stem from a physiocratic value system, not actual grievances. It could not be otherwise; unless relegated to myth, the agrarian position on labor would suggest that Populism responded to the present, not the past. In fact, the retrogressive framework creates such a strong presumption against the existence of farmer-labor ties that it has actually discouraged the gathering of data in this direction. Only one student of agrarian radicalism, Chester McArthur Destler, seriously entertained the idea of further exploration.

And his findings on the ideological interaction and attempts at coalition between the two groups do indeed cast doubt on the framework. Yet, significantly, there is such a manifest unwillingness to think in these terms that later scholars did not follow up Destler's investigations. Had he not published, ample reason would still exist for suspecting that farmers and workers sought joint organization during this period. The two decades preceding Populism, which saw the rise of the Greenback movement and the Knights of Labor, bear out this contention.[4]

Thus, sufficient evidence *already* had been accumulated in the areas of technology, politics, and industrial labor to reject the retrogressive framework as contrary to fact. Still, it must be emphasized that under ordinary circumstances there would be little need to raise the issue. Except for stifling research into farmer-labor activity, the framework has not proven injurious; and except for preventing the requisite level of abstraction needed to bring American materials into comparative perspective with those of other industrial societies, it has not even been a disadvantage. Why, then, if the facts of earlier studies can stand alone, should any consideration be given to the distinction between progressive and retrogressive? The question takes on increased significance when it is recalled that earlier writers did not usually permit the framework to interfere with basic research. In fact, these studies of Populism—not only those of Hicks and Destler, but the state analyses of Ernest D. Stewart, Alex M. Arnett, Herman C. Nixon, Hallie Farmer, Raymond Miller, and others—are among the finest monographic writing in American historiography. Hence, the reason for pursuing the matter lies elsewhere than in the adequacy of previous scholarship. Instead, the issue is crucial today because the retrogressive framework has recently become an end in itself, even to the extent that it jeopardizes the existence of earlier works by obscuring their factual content. It is not too much to say that the issue concerns nothing less than the place of Populism in American history.

Ignoring what came before, proponents of this framework adopt the following line of reasoning: Populism did not adjust to industrialism; hence, the movement occupied an untenable historical position. And because it looked backward, its long-range solutions were, by definition, unrealistic. This meant that by not comprehending the basis for its discontent, Populism was forced to search for simplistic explanations and, ultimately, scapegoats. The result is a cumulatively deteriorating position; as protest becomes more emotional, it bears less resemblance to reality. The final image is that of a movement of opportunists, crackpots, and anti-Semites, whose perception of the world conforms to the dictates of a conspiracy theory of history. The over-all consequence of this image is that Populism has been denied its traditional place as a democratic social force. Rather, its significance for American history is altered so greatly that it has come to stand as the source for later proto-fascist groups, McCarthyism, anti-Semitism, xenophobia, and anti-intellectualism. One senses the proportions of this denigration process when it is seen that the very term "populistic" has passed into the working vocabulary of many intellectuals as an epithet, signifying the traits just enumerated.[5]

The final dissociation of this image from previous scholarship occurs over the question of social conditions during the 1890's. Earlier writers never challenged the fact of hard times. Rather, they took Populist protest seriously as a direct response to economic grievances. It would be well to recall the situation facing Populism, as found in Hicks and other standard accounts: the serious decline in farm prices during the period 1870–1897; the railroad rate structure and, perhaps as important, railroad land and tax policies; high mortgage indebtedness within a financial context of contracting currency; actual dispossession from the land; adverse marketing arrangements, particularly the power of elevator companies to fix prices and establish grading standards; and consumption in a monopolistic framework.

The new image of Populism, by emphasizing irrationality, shifts the responsibility for discontent away from society and to Populism itself: The movement was more rhetorical than radical; hence, its protest was grossly exaggerated. Following this through, proponents of this view held that Populism was not a trustworthy barometer for reflecting actual conditions. The result was that the extent of oppression became increasingly minimized, and finally glossed over. And because the basis for discontent was almost totally denied, Populism then became subject to the charge of double irrationality: Not only was it retrogressive, but it responded to nonexistent grievances. Meanwhile, the society which gave birth to the protest was forgotten or exonerated.

Given the consequences of this framework, the task at hand must be a study directed incisively to the core of the present discussion—the distinction between retrogressive and progressive social forces. Another general history of Populism is unnecessary. Frankly, one cannot surpass Hicks on the politics of the movement, for his work is replete with election statistics, verbatim platforms, and convention proceedings. Nor should one dwell on the historical foundations of Populism. There is an extensive literature on protest movements and, equally important, on agricultural organizations for the 1870's and 1880's. It is sufficient to note here that Populism did not develop in a vacuum, dating from the St. Louis Demands of 1889 to Election Day, 1896. Rather, it was the culmination of a unified development, beginning with Grangerism and Greenbackism in the early 1870's. This fact is borne out by the movement's composition: Leaders and rank-and-file alike consistently appear throughout the period in the successive third-party attempts. Thus, it would be futile to retrace the steps of earlier students. Instead, a fresh approach is in order, *but* one grounded firmly on the bedrock of primary sources.

I shall therefore present an intellectual history of midwestern Populism, tracing its response to industrial America through evidence fully nine-tenths of which has never before appeared. There are important limitations, of course, in confining the analysis to the midwest, for one cannot then generalize regarding the entire Populist movement. When it is recognized that the south was as influential in certain aspects of Populism, the necessary qualifications will suggest themselves to the reader. This holds to a lesser extent for other regions as well. Yet, even here one finds a distinct advantage in restricting the scope: a more crystallized form of the relation between industrialism and agrarian radicalism than might otherwise be possible.

My sources are Populist manuscripts and newspapers contained in the state historical societies of Minnesota, Nebraska, Wisconsin, and Kansas, and several collections located elsewhere. The evidence is presented with an eye to capturing the underlying currents of Populism. Here the movement suddenly springs to life, not as a set of proposals but as the despair and yearning of the people themselves. When seen through the words of unlettered farmers and workers, Populism ceases to be an abstraction; instead, movement and rank-and-file become fused into one. While the views of leaders invariably predominate in such sources, one also finds the account of a so-called "tramp" seeking work, the angry editorials of a Broken Bow newspaper, or the resignation of an Arizona farmer's wife recently thrown off the land in Kansas. I have emphasized, so far as the materials would permit, evidence of this more representative character. Under the circumstances, it seemed inadvisable to make use of the customary *sic;* instead, the evidence is reproduced as in the original. .

The grass-roots world of Populism is thereby opened, revealing what for me was an exciting dimension. A kind of folk-wisdom emerges, which grasps complex philosophic questions and pierces to their heart with deceptively simple solutions. The reason behind this, while perhaps mystifying to the intellectual, is not hard to seek. Populists lived these problems, drawing their answers from experience itself. Nor were these trivial questions. As will become clear, Populism formulated an extraordinarily penetrating critique of industrial society.

Sensing that man was becoming dehumanized, in psychological as well as economic terms, it recognized the trend toward what we today call alienation. And this was not a Ruskinesque lament for an outmoded handicraft existence. On the contrary, Populism made the important distinction between technology and social context, holding that society perverted the productive forces through a maldistribution of wealth. But I am getting ahead of the story. Let it suffice that Populism is regarded here as a mirror of America, and its criticism, a reflection of social conditions during the 1890's.

Yet, a problem of methodology remains. A danger almost intrinsic to intellectual history is that ideas will become divorced from their setting and be viewed in isolation. The present study, because it presupposes so much of the necessary context, is clearly no exception. Hence, one must write intellectual history with serious reservations in mind, notably that ideas do not always reveal a movement's social composition or its economic foundation. While perhaps oversensitive to these difficulties, I believe the intellectual history of social movements is without value unless the evidence is in fact representative. Once this criterion has been satisfied, however, the next step becomes possible: to view intellectual history as a creative and highly *positive* tool, capable not only of supplementing other approaches but of clarifying the factors of economy and social structure usually ruled outside its province.

This last statement does not reverse my initial skepticism; it merely suggests that intellectual history can, in practice, bridge the gulf between ideas and their social roots. The present study is itself an example of this extremely interesting feedback effect: Evidence is found which cannot be explained in terms of prevailing notions; then, instead of discarding the evidence, one is forced to entertain new hypotheses; finally, by working backward from the ideas, one discovers hitherto neglected aspects within the movement. My own position was developed precisely in this way. Starting the research with the preconceptions of previous writers, including the retrogressive framework, I began to note what at the time seemed contrary straws in the wind: an Alliance in Nebraska endorsing Coxey's army, a militant labor leader praising the proclamation of a Kansas Populist governor, and a Socialist Labor Party organizer complaining that Populism stole potential recruits. Slowly the details fell into place. The process is described here to show that my interpretation, however controversial, grows directly out of the evidence itself. It was reached inductively, and not deductively. If the dramatis personae appear strange—intellectuals and workers, as well as farmers—this is a testimony to the possibilities of intellectual history.

I propose, then, the following historical definition of midwestern Populism: While primarily an agrarian movement, it also contained significant support from industrial labor, social reformers, and intellectuals. The interaction between these groups was expressed not in terms of pre-industrial producer values, but of a common ideology stemming from a shared critique of existing conditions. In a word, Populism regarded itself as a class movement, reasoning that farmers and workers were assuming the same material position in society. Thus, it accepted industrialism but opposed its capitalistic form, seeking instead a more equitable distribution of wealth. But Populism went further in its criticism: Industrial capitalism not only impoverished the individual, it alienated and degraded him. The threat was not only subsistence living, but the destruction of human faculties. According to Populism, there was an inverse relation between industrialism and freedom, because the machine was being made to exploit rather than serve man. Is Populism, then, a socialist movement? Here labels become unimportant; it was far more radical than is generally assumed. Had Populism succeeded, it could have fundamentally altered American society in a socialist direction. Clearly, Populism was a progressive social force.

✣

CHAPTER ONE

"... THE FULLNESS
OF THE DIVINITY
OF HUMANITY"

Populism had a peculiar notion of freedom: Man was free only when society encouraged the fullest possible development of human potentiality. Addressing the mammoth Tattersall rally, which climaxed the 1894 People's party campaign in Chicago, Henry Demarest Lloyd declared: "The people's party is more than the organized discontent of the people. It is the organized aspiration of the people for a fuller, nobler, richer, kindlier life for every man, woman, and child in the ranks of humanity." Seeking to enhance human self-fulfillment, it could not be a temporary phenomenon: "The people's party is not a passing cloud on the political sky. It is not a transient gust of popular discontent caused by bad crops or hard times." Rather, "It is an uprising of principle, and the millions who have espoused these principles will not stop until they have become incorporated into the constitution of the government and the framework of society." Thus, the goal of Populism was "the hope of realizing and incarnating in the lives of the common people the fullness of the divinity of humanity." [1]

WINGATE COLLEGE LIBRARY
WINGATE, N. C.

Here, then, was a standard for judging industrial America in the 1890's: Did it promote "the divinity of humanity," or merely produce dehumanized and impoverished men? While human rights is an abstraction admirably suited to campaign rhetoric, the theme recurs with sufficient frequency and intensity to indicate that Populists took it seriously. As Hamlin Garland stated to James B. Weaver, in the midst of the latter's 1892 presidential campaign: "Don't confine the fight to any one thing money or land. Let's make the fight for *human liberty* and for the rights of man." Ignatius Donnelly, in a circular prepared for party members in the 1896 campaign, defined the task at hand as "the preservation of humanity in the highest estate of which it is capable on earth." And Senator Allen of Nebraska similarly held that Populism "rests on the cause of labor and the brotherhood of man." [2]

Populists further clarified their conception of human rights by distinguishing it from property rights. Governor Lorenzo D. Lewelling of Kansas, in a major speech, reminded his Kansas City audience that "we have so much regard for the rights of property that we have forgotten the liberties of the individual." A Broken Bow, Nebraska, paper saw the conflict as that of the "rights of man" and the "rights of capital." And one in Nelson, Nebraska, characterized it as between "the wealthy and powerful classes who want the control of the government to plunder the people" and "the people" themselves, who are "contending for equality before the law and the rights of man." [3]

More concretely, human rights are a sham unless predicated upon an equitable distribution of wealth. An editorial in the, Lincoln, Nebraska, *Farmers' Alliance* expressed the view in these words: "The people's party has sprung into existence not to make the black man free, but to emancipate all men; not to secure political freedom to a class, but to gain for all *industrial* freedom, without which there can be no political freedom; no lasting people's government." Making "industrial freedom" the precondition for political freedom, it further asserted that the People's party "stands upon the declaration that 'all men are created equal,' having equal right to live, labor and enjoy the fruits of their labor. It teaches that none should have power to enjoy without labor." On the contrary, Populism "demands equal opportunities and exact justice in business for each individual and proposes to abolish all monopolistic privileges and power." Thus, the perspective is refined still further: Monopoly poses the principal threat to human rights. Significantly, the editorial immediately added that the People's party "is the first party that has comprehended the great question of injustice and proposed an adequate remedy for the evils of society." Its closing sentence reveals that, while opposing monopoly, Populism accepted industrialism: Populists "shall make of this nation an industrial democracy in which each citizen shall have an equal interest." [4]

At the same Tattersall rally where Lloyd spoke, Clarence Darrow also called for a more democratic industrial system: "We of the People's party believe that the men who created our wonderful industrial system have the right to enjoy the institution which they have created." A Columbus, Nebraska, paper voiced the same sentiment: "The people do not want to tear up the railroads nor pull down the factories." Instead,, "they want to build up and make better everything." And social protest became necessary to secure these conditions, for "even a worm will writhe and struggle when stepped upon, and surely, if Americans cannot be anything higher, they can be a nation of worms." As the Populist organ in Wahoo, Nebraska, simply observed: "There should be no want." Thus, industrial America could, but did not, provide greater material benefits for the total society. The technological potential was present for overcoming poverty, the results otherwise. A correspondent to Lloyd summarized this feeling when he wrote: "The whole ideal of our civilization is wrong." [5]

But privation was not inevitable; measures *could* be taken to create a more equitable distribution of wealth. Here the essential rationality of Populism becomes clear: Man could rationally control his society, particularly by harnessing the productive forces already in existence. But this could not occur under the existing form of social organization, for industrial capitalism was not responsive to human needs. Society, in a word, had to be changed. And while the means selected were moderate —working through the political system—this should not obscure the radical conception Populists maintained of politics. The same Columbus paper defined politics as the ability to control "the distribution of wealth." Politics no longer meant seeking office, still less preserving the status quo. Rather, this paper added, "Politics can cause this country to bloom and blossom like the rose; it can make our people, generally speaking, prosperous, happy and contented, or it can stagnate every kind of enterprise, reduce the masses to want and misery and cause our people to become restless, desperate and blood-thirsty." [6]

Frank Doster, a Populist leader in Kansas, spelled out in detail this demand for political action to achieve the benefits of technology. Speaking at Topeka on Labor Day of 1894, Doster pointed out that although "steam, electricity, compressed air, are utilized to do the work of man," the expected gains failed to materialize. These productive forces, which are "the common property of all," have not benefited the total society because they "have been made the monopoly of the few." Through this monopoly structure they "have been turned aside from the beneficent ends for which designed, to serve the selfish purposes of avarice and greed." Moreover, Populism was, according to Doster, the only major political force which sought to control economic concentration in the interests of the larger society: "In the face of the power exerted by the monopolists of these tremendous engines of industry and commerce the republican and democratic parties stand paralyzed—hypnotized, as it were, unable to control it or give direction and shape for common good." Here the traditional charge is reversed; a Populist holds that the major parties have been overwhelmed by these rapid changes. "The failure to adapt the legislation of the country to the strange conditions which this new life has forced upon us is the cause in greater part of our industrial ills." The statement suggests the attempt to confront, not retreat from, the new situation. Accordingly, Doster closed with a presentation of "two political formulae," serving as the "philosophic bases" for reliance upon governmental action: Government must "do that for the individual which he can not successfully do for himself, and which other individuals will not do for him upon just and equitable terms." And more comprehensively, "the industrial system of a nation, like its political system, should be a government of and for and by the people alone." [7]

Stepping back momentarily to view Populist thought in a wider ideological spectrum, one immediately recognizes its challenge to what are generally considered the prevailing ideologies of the period—the success myth, social Darwinism, and laissez faire. Governor Lewelling's Kansas City speech clearly states the Populist case for paternalism: "It is the business of the Government to make it possible for me to live and sustain the life of my family." Further, "It is the duty of government to protect the weak, because the strong are able to protect themselves." This is totally at variance with the success-myth faith in individual self-help through character development, industry, and perseverance. An article in the *Farmers' Alliance* suggests why Populists could not subscribe to the success myth: It contradicted their actual experiences, denied their grievances, and led to markedly different conclusions regarding the operation of the economic system. Hence, "No effort of the people, no degree of economy, no amount of industry in their several avocations could have averted these results. The people are as powerless as though they were actually in a state of bondage." A change in the nature of society, not a reliance on individual self-help, was necessary: "While the cause exists the evils *must* and *will* remain." [8]

But Populism rejected the success myth, and indeed laissez faire and social Darwinism, for a more basic reason. Unbridled individualism, it contended, destroyed rather than promoted the general welfare. Its own counter-formulation, simply, was that cooperation and mutual help, not competition and self-help, led to true individualism.

An editorial in the *Farmers' Alliance* stated the argument as follows: "The plutocracy of to-day is the logical result of the individual freedom which we have always considered the pride of our system." In fact, "The theory of our government has been and is that the individual should possess the very greatest degree of liberty consistent, not with the greatest good of the greatest number, but with the very least legal restraint compatible with law and order. Individual enterprise was allowed unlimited scope." Thus, individualism creates monopoly capitalism, where "the corporation has absorbed the community." Instead, the reverse must take place: "The community must now absorb the corporation—must merge itself into it. Society must enlarge itself to the breadth of humanity." The editorial closed with an unmistakable repudiation of these other value systems: "A stage must be reached in which each will be for all and all for each. The welfare of the individual must be the object and end of all effort." And three years later, this paper (under its new name, *Alliance-Independent*) succinctly noted that "a reigning plutocracy with the masses enslaved, is the natural development and end of individualism." It remained for the Topeka *Advocate* to add a final, somewhat ironic, comment: "The horror of 'paternalism' hangs like a black pall over the burried hopes of the helpless poor." [9]

Populism was even more unsparing in its criticism of

social Darwinism, especially the latter's sanction of competition and survival of the fittest. Governor Lewelling, again in the Kansas City speech, warned that unless the government exerted greater control over industrial capitalism there would be "a state of barbarism and everywhere we slay, and the slayer in turn is slain and so on the great theatre of life is one vast conspiracy all creatures from the worm to the man in turn rob their fellows." For him, social Darwinism meant "the law of natural selection the survival of the fittest—Not the survival of the fittest, but the survival of the strongest." Lewelling concluded: "It is time that man should rise above it." [10]

George H. Gibson, in a letter to the *Alliance-Independent* (he later became its editor), expressed a similar view of competition. Arguing that the type of social reform represented by Jane Addams was futile, he observed: "Uplifting the masses is all right, but it would be much better to put a stop to the beastly struggle which crowds them down." Nor did Gibson reason abstractly; he denied the wisdom of competition by what was daily taking place in American society. "There are tens of thousands in this city [Chicago] all the time out of work, fighting for positions and the low wages which enable capitalists to rake off dividends for idle and scheming stockholders." Writing later to Henry D. Lloyd, Gibson outlined his counter-proposal to competition: "We must put together our property, labor, economic wisdom, knowledge, varying talents, Christianizing or democratizing what we have and are . . . We feel that it is wrong to continue the selfish struggle, even with charitable or philanthropic intent, as many noble souls are doing." [11]

Using for his standard "political and economic equality," a Walnut Grove, Minnesota, editor judged competitive society in these terms: "The calamities that have heretofore and that now are upon us—as a nation—are but the measure or indicator of the extent that this standard has been departed from in the practice of the competitive system." Nor did Populists admire those who were presumably the fittest. Ignatius Donnelly characterized them as follows: "Shallow-pated, sordid, unintellectual, they stand there, grabbing and grinning, while their brethren march past them to destruction." The Columbus, Nebraska, paper was less charitable, describing "the so-called great men" as "moral cowards and public plunderers" who have "reversed the code of morals and stand up like hypocrites of olden times and thank god they are not like other men are." And it opposed these men, again not on abstract grounds, but because it regarded competition as destroying all but the victors: "They have the power to impoverish the farmers, make millions of good men tramps; to reduce their employees to silent slaves; to ruin great cities; to plunge a happy and prosperous nation into sorrow and bankruptcy." [12]

These criticisms do not, however, reflect a conspiracy theory of history; Populists were concerned with the consequences of power, not the personalities or motivations of successful men. Referring to Rockefeller, Henry D. Lloyd noted that personal questions are extraneous because "the main point is the simple issue of monopoly." Even if "they are angels," he continued, the problem remains critical so long as they "have obtained the power of controlling the markets." Lloyd argued somewhat earlier in this same fashion against Carnegie, "I have no sort of feeling" against the man, but he is nonetheless "one of the worst representatives of our mercenary system of ordering industry which is perverting it from the supply of demand and the production and distribution of the wealth in nature for the use of all men, and making it an instrument of personal aggrandisement and cannibalistic selfishness." [13]

Nor did Populism concede the more attractive side of social Darwinism, the latter's belief that society evolved into progressively higher stages. Technological progress was one matter—its translation into material well-being quite another. "While we think, brag of it, how far we are ahead of any former civilization," wrote a Minnesota state senator to Donnelly, "I for one am disgusted of the bragging and boasting and simply believe it is not true." Surely, through improvements in communications, "we are making history a little faster than when those elements were lacking in the worlds affairs." But, he added, "I disdain to call it progress when, considering what it eventually . . . will lead to." This position is exceedingly interesting, for it starts from the recognition that technology provides the means for the liberation of man: "I have heard it asserted that the printing Press, telegraph, etc. have educated the masses, that the direful relapse will not come again as in the past." Yet, he then reaches a decidedly unexpected conclusion. While it can serve man, technology can also be used to insure a greater domination over man. In a word, progress is not only meaningless for a defective society; it actually becomes harmful by intensifying these defects. For Populism, then, progress was not an unmixed blessing: "Bosh, our would be masters have a corner on the whole outfit of the inventions, and they are now just as much employed to the destruction of human rights as formerly in the absence of those inventions the peoples ignorance was used as a means." [14]

Yet, Populism denied not the idea of progress but its realization in existing society. Optimistic in reforming zeal, Populism was still essentially pessimistic in its awareness of the ensuing obstacles. Not surprisingly, the result was an ambivalence with pessimism the overriding factor. A letter to Bryan after the 1896 election stated that an "appeal to reason may elevate the human race to a point we dream not of." But the same letter tempered this optimistic outburst with a sobering reminder: "A social system which permits puny children to toil in grimy factories and foul sweatshops while brawny men walk the streets vainly begging for work . . . is damnable!" How, then, could the net balance be otherwise than on the pessimistic side when Populists continually asked themselves such questions as this: "And for what object has this tremendous slaughter of the human family and this unparalleled suffering of the living been inflicted upon mankind?" [15]

Thus, Populism did not subscribe to the ideologies of individualism, competition, and progress. But its response, far from being negative, was to redefine entirely the relation between society and the individual. Contrary to Populism, the other three ideologies held the individual alone responsible for his plight; perseverance, ruthlessness, or industry determined one's position in the social structure. Populism reversed this: society itself was blamed for human impoverishment. The way was therefore cleared for social protest. No longer was man thrown back upon his imagined inadequacies; self-recrimination and additional frenetic activity were rejected as guides to improving one's life-situation. Atomized man gave way to social man, individual responsibility to social responsibility. Society, not the individual, had to be changed. Indeed, Populism was the major radical alternative of this period.

✤

CHAPTER TWO

TRAMPS AND VAGABONDS
Signs of the Time

Populism criticized industrial America for creating not only poverty but a new man—alienated man. With economic hardship there came a marked change in man's psychological condition; physical degradation was destroying his sense of being human. "The materialism of to-day," began a *Farmers' Alliance* editorial, "does all the time seggregate human lives." Thus, man was becoming divorced from himself and from others. Nor was the reason hard to seek: "Take a man for instance, who labors hard from fourteen to sixteen hours a day to obtain the bare necessaries of life. He eats his bacon and potatoes in a place which might rather be called a den than a home: and then, worn out, lies down and sleeps." The product of this less than human existence was a less than human man: "He is brutalized both morally and physically. He has no ideas, only propensities. He has no beliefs, only instincts. He does not, often cannot, read." But there was even more at stake than the loss of human faculties. The individual was becoming subordinated both to the dominant groups in society and to the productive system itself: "His contact with other people is only the relation of servant to master, of a machine to its director." The editorial then asked a question which captures the very essence of the Populist critique of industrial society: "How can you reach this man, how kindle the divine spark which is torpid in his soul, when he knows that it is greed that enforces the material labor that is crushing him down, when he feels it is the wage system that is stealing the fruits of his toil and abasing and enslaving him?"

Moreover, this was a world trend, not a temporary phenomenon: "Here is Humanity's problem. It involves all other problems, and all modern life. . . This man's name is Million. He is all about us. He constitutes half the population of the world." The reference, clearly, is to industrial capitalism. "How is he to have more time and more energy to develop his faculties except by lessening his hours of labor and increasing his wages?" Significantly, the solution offered, in the form of three additional questions, is not concerned with partial reform; the system itself must be fundamentally altered: "Can this be done under the present system? Has there been a better system in the world? Does not the problem of humanity demand that there shall be a better system?" Leaving no doubt as to its meaning, the editorial emphatically added: "There *must* be a better one."

Maintaining, next, that the existing system was based upon competition, it pointed to the hollow social relations which resulted: "The tendency of the competitive system is to antagonize and disassociate men." And this basic inhumanity was reflected through the ethos of industrial society: "The survival of the fittest is a satanic creed, applicable to the savage creation, perhaps, but only in the broadest sense to men." These tendencies must be halted; man must reassert the fact that he is still man. "Humanity must rise to its own needs or the soul of man will flee, and the senses be left alone to reign." Thus, competition is nothing less than war itself, the final denigration of man: "The actual state of society to-day is a state of war, active irreconcilable war on every side, and in all things. Deny it if you can. Competition is only another name for war." The result can only mean "slavery to millions," and to "thousands upon thousands starvation, misery and death." The closing lines perhaps best express not only the radicalism but the earnestness of this position: "After four thousand years of life is this the best that we can achieve? If so, who cares how soon the end may come?" [1]

The separate aspects of this critique now assume some cohesion: Human rights are denied by existing society; only a basic change—the stress on paternalism and "industrial democracy"—can overcome this condition. In the preceding two years the *Farmers' Alliance* had carefully developed this position, stating flatly in one editorial that contemporary conditions on their face constituted "sufficient evidence that the whole system under which they have lived is a lie and an imposture." Because the "people have produced but they possess not," it continued, these very conditions of hardship were progressively worsening: "The present cruelly unjust system, therefore, is fast working the hopeless pauperization and degradation of the toiling masses." [2]

And on another occasion the newspaper suggested why Populism itself must initiate the necessary changes. While the dominant groups in American society "might consent to congress doing something temporary for the relief of the people," they will never permit, in fact will strongly resist, any measure affecting the structure of that society. Hence, "As for interfering with the system which they have for so long been gradually bringing about, they will NEVER consent to that." Partial amelioration was therefore futile, for "without a complete eradication of this system the people cannot for once hope for relief of a permanent character." Three years later, still pursuing the argument that human degradation had economic roots, the paper posed this question: "Now what is life and so-called liberty if the means of subsistence are monopolized?" Its reply hints at the more systematic economic analysis to come: "Hunger-scourged the dependent laborers must accept wages that independent employers choose to offer, and the wages are made so low that the dependent cannot become independent." Implying a state of permanent subjugation, it added that "more are reduced to dependence than rise to independence." [3]

For Populism dependent man was not a flowery abstraction but an economic fact; industrial society transformed the individual into a commodity. Lloyd expressed this view when, in a letter to Samuel Gompers, he described Carnegie as "perhaps the most conspicuous representative of the wage system . . . which holds the laborer to be merely a commodity to be cheapened to the last cent." Nor was this accidental; man as commodity signified both a coercive process and the defining tendency of the economic system: "Carnegie can be used to teach the captains of Industry that men who treat their 'brother' laborers like sponges to be squeezed and rats to be shot cannot continue doing business in that style in this country." [4]

Specifically, wages were driven to the subsistence level in order to increase profits, regardless of the attendant social consequences. "It is in the interest of the capitalist class," contended the *Farmers' Alliance*, "to have as many men as possible out of work and seeking it in order to keep and force wages down by making competition fierce between those seeking work and those employed." Here the Populist labor theory of value becomes meaningful. That the producer should receive the benefit of his labor is not a throwback to rural utopia but a highly positive critique aimed directly at the profit system. "The heresy of present economic teaching," this same paper noted, "is the idea that 'profit,' more labor for less labor, is a good thing and to be taken whenever it can be obtained." The principle at stake was not an equitable return for labor; it was profit itself: "It is this heresy which dethrones justice, perpetuates war, destroys the commercial equilibrium, makes the seller unable to buy back as much labor value as he sold, and so leads to glutted markets." In a word, "the workers are in constant want." [5]

Thus, profit and subsistence living were intertwined. "The men who work for wages," observed the *Alliance-Independent*, "must earn their wages and more, that is, a profit for their employers; and if a capitalist stands behind the employer the wage-earner must earn another profit for him." As a result, the profit system "has given to the usurer or monopolist class power to buy up land, capital railroads, mines, etc., and to so increase their power to the people's dependence." The surplus worker,

according to the *Farmers' Alliance*, makes possible this
system of profit and subsistence: "The army of destitute
unemployed is the source of its power, the misery of the
unemployed is the club with which it enslaves all workers." [6]

The Topeka *Advocate* went further: industrial capitalism manipulated technology to create a surplus labor
force. The *Advocate* began with this question: "Has
society, as a whole, derived the benefits from the use of
labor-saving machinery that it might have done under a
different system?" It replied, "We think not. Under the
prevailing system the capitalist has been the chief beneficiary." Not the machine but its utilization was at fault:
"Instead of using it to displace men, it should have been
used to reduce the hours of labor." The creation of
superfluous men is wholly unnecessary; more people
could be employed at shorter hours, "thereby continuing
the opportunities of all to provide the comforts and
luxuries of life for every member of society." In fact, the
very potentiality of technology serves as a critical standard for measuring the injustice of society: "Let us admit,
for our present purpose, that there is more of everything
produced than the necessities of the people require. The
fact that all are not supplied, then, shows that there is
something wrong in our system." The paper urged,
"Look at the multitudes who have been but recently
thrown out of employment, and whose families have
been destitute in consequence." The success myth will
not do; these are social problems, and society itself must
be held responsible. "It is cruel, it is inhuman, to attribute
these conditions to laziness, drunkenness and incompe-
tency. They are the natural product of a false and vicious

system by which the few grow rich beyond all human need, and the many are doomed to eternal poverty and want."

This it called simply the "modern condition," the quality of life in industrial America: "One of the causes of this 'modern condition' is the monopoly of machinery and other means of production and distribution by which the few are benefited and the many are deprived of fair opportunities in life." One need only compare society as it is and might be to grasp the painful disparity. "Contrast this 'modern condition' with what might be attained by a proper use of the instrumentalities of modern production and distribution." Here the Populist faith in technology emerges; society *can* overcome alienated man—if only industrialism were to exist in a more democratic framework. When "work should be so distributed that each should do his share and receive the reward of his labor," then man can finally enter a new realm of existence. Society would promote not dwarf his intellectual as well as material development, for "the time not required for such production should be devoted to rest, to mental culture, to social intercourse and recreation." [7]

Thus, technology was not intrinsically repressive; it was neutral, society alone determining whether it served or exploited man. "Under the existing monopoly system of industry," the *Advocate* stated one year later, "capital owns and controls all this labor-saving machinery, and derives all the benefits resulting from its use, while labor is forced into idleness and compelled to beg, steal or starve." Paternalism naturally followed. But society, as then constituted, refused to correct these abuses: "At the same time we are told that state and national governments are powerless to provide employment to these enforced idlers or assist them in any way to supply the necessities of themselves and families, because to do so would be paternalism." The paper's own reaction to the charge was simply, "Isn't it a system to be proud of?" Nor was the question unimportant. Populism recognized both the implications of its critique and the way society would seek to discredit it as irrational: "Every person who has the temerity to suggest that changes are possible by which a better state of society might be secured, is denounced as an impractical visionary and a crank." [8]

But Populism did more than anticipate its critics. Taking the offensive, it countered that society was far from sacrosanct. No amount of sophistry would disguise the fact that this was an age of brutality. Thus, society must be exposed for what it had made of man. Its worst features must be analyzed because these, far from being atypical, revealed the innermost core of industrial capitalism. Nor was this a concern with the sordid for its own sake; that society permitted *any* abuse of man was ample testimony to its defective structure. Further, these abuses were a direct reflection of prevailing institutions; their very existence defined the goal of society. Alienated man therefore *was* industrial America. Clarence Darrow summed up this view in a letter to Lloyd: "Do you know that they are making history very fast in America and all the history is against freedom." [9]

One fact, one living reality, came to symbolize the pervading degradation and hardship: the unemployed who wandered alone or joined the industrial armies. Governor Lewelling comprehensively stated the problem in an executive proclamation of December 1893, referred to by contemporaries as the "Tramp Circular." Drawing the analogy between conditions in Elizabethan England, pre-revolutionary France, and America in the 1890's, Lewelling held that each of these societies underwent precisely the same formative experience. Men were uprooted from independent positions and transformed into surplus labor—into so-called tramps and vagabonds. Hence, the foundation of industrial society was progressively increasing poverty—the unemployed.

For England, "in the reign of Elizabeth, the highways were filled with the throngs of the unemployed poor, who were made to 'move on,' and were sometimes brutally whipped, sometimes summarily hanged, as 'sturdy vagrants' or 'incorrigible vagabonds.' " The same social process occurred in France, where "just previous to the revolution, the punishment of being poor and out of work was, for the first offense, a term of years in the galleys, for the second offense, the galleys for life." And in America, "the monopoly of labor saving machinery and its devotion to selfish instead of social use, have rendered more and more human beings superfluous, until we have a standing army of the unemployed numbering even in the most prosperous times not less than one million able bodied men."

Here the Populist critique attains its fullest form: Intrinsic to capitalist development is superfluous man. Again, the success myth and individual responsibility are denied. Superfluous man emphatically is not lazy and immoral man: "Yet, until recently it was the prevailing notion, as it is yet the notion of all but the work-people themselves and those of other classes given to thinking,

and whosoever, being able bodied and willing to work
can always find work to do." Then the immediate issue
is raised. Lewelling attacked a Kansas statute enacted to
punish the impoverished: "The man out of work and
penniless is, by this legislation, classed with 'confidence
men.'" Implying a comparison with English and French
predecessors, Lewelling maintained that through this
statute "thousands of men, guilty of no crime but poverty, intent upon no crime but that of seeking employment, have languished in the city prisons of Kansas or
performed unrequited toil on 'rock piles' as municipal
slaves, because ignorance of economic conditions had
made us cruel."

Once more paternalism directly follows; society itself
makes this view imperative. "But those who sit in the
seats of power are bound by the highest obligation to
especially regard the cause of the oppressed and helpless
poor." Hence, "the first duty of the government is to
the weak. Power becomes fiendish if it be not the pro-
tector and sure reliance of the friendless, to whose com-
plaints all other ears are deaf." The statute, then, is clearly aimed at the lower classes: "And who needs to be told
that equal protection of the laws does not prevail where
this inhuman vagrancy law is enforced?" The result is
the increased helplessness of the lower classes: "It sepa-
rates men into two distinct classes, differentiated as those
who are penniless and those who are not, and declare
the former criminals. Only the latter are entitled to the
liberty guaranteed by the constitution." Further, the
statute punishes the very groups society itself created;
poverty becomes legalized, and subordination the permanent condition. "To be found in a city 'without some

visible means of support or some legitimate business,' is the involuntary condition of some millions at this moment, and we proceed to punish them for being victims of conditions which we, as a people, have forced upon them." Lewelling quietly concluded, "Let simple poverty cease to be a crime." [10]

Clearly, Lewelling halted before reaching the logical next step: the eradication, not humane treatment, of poverty. Yet, the moderate tone is not surprising; this was a directive to metropolitan police commissioners, and not a philosophic statement. But its significance was not lost to contemporaries. Populism saw the "Tramp Circular" as a manifesto indicting society for its brutality.

"Governor Lewelling is the first and only man in authority," Eugene V. Debs wrote in the *Locomotive Firemen's Magazine*, "to brand the cruel, savage, heartless wrongs in fitting terms." Debs then posed the central question for Populism: "Governor Lewelling's letter ought, in the very nature of things, to arouse everywhere the inquiry in this country: why are there so many tramps?" The Topeka *Advocate*, at times spokesman for Lewelling, discussed the proclamation in detail. Conditions creating tramps are inexcusable, it observed, "not because they are new, but because they are entirely unnecessary," given the country's "unlimited resources." The tramp therefore was "the result of our vicious social and economic system." But society not only gave birth to the tramp, it continually renewed his dependency: "Idleness is enforced in consequence of vicious and discriminating laws, and to treat the helpless victims of these unnatural conditions as criminals is itself a crime against which every instinct of humanity revolts." By suggesting

the comparability of European and American development, the *Advocate* implied the solution absent from the
proclamation: "Is poverty more tolerable in one age than
in another? Are the poor of America poor from choice
any more than were those in the reign of Queen Elizabeth, or in France under a 'dissolute monarchy?' Is a
dissolute monarchy any worse than a dissolute republic?"
Three weeks later this paper answered: "Remember that
tramps are men, and that they are a natural product of
our social system." The discussion was concluded with
an even more emphatic plea for basic change: "There
must be discovered some way to deal with them consistently with these facts. Can it be done without a
revolution of our system? We think not." [11]

Lewelling's correspondents also placed the issue in a
larger context; simply, society created the tramp. "The
tendency of the times," a North Wichita man wrote,
"is to force the masses into a propertyless condition, then
persecute them for vagabondage." Another saw the
tramp as the natural outcome of a society where "the
dollar, instead of humanity," is "the object of the su-
premest regard and protection." Fear now gripped the
people; they wondered when their turn would come:
"*Who* does *not* bear constantly with him the dark
spector, that by another year perhaps he and his may be
vagrants; and does not each succeeding year give to the
word a deeper and more damning dye." More important,
the very existence of tramps signified a crisis in capitalist
development: "Are not wrong principles and courses,
if persisted in, cumulative in volume and results? Is not
now, a pivotal time of the *ripening* forces of many cen-
turies?" The present, this writer added, marked "a pivot-

al or turning point in time . . . when every element for good or *evil* is *developed to a* ripened maturity of forces."

Thus, the tramp was more than a sign of the time; he reflected through his own person the tendencies of industrial society. He symbolized, for Populism, the approaching crisis. Industrial America had reached maturity and a juncture in social development; it could continue its present course or veer in a more democratic direction. The 1890's would decide the fate of human rights—but that decision was now; once fully organized, society would prevent all future social protest. Hence, the intensity of Populism. This was a watershed in history; the principle of freedom itself was at stake. The letter concluded on that very note: "When may not a little more universality of privation and hunger inaugerate a universal riot and there be a *positive* want of supply, instead of only want of unequal distribution?" The problem, then, was not an isolated penal statute but the future of society: "I believe governor you see the iminence of all this in the near future." [12]

Other letters attached the same meaning to the proclamation, one calling it a protest "against the growing tendency" to class legislation, which "while closing up the channels of prosperity against the poor treats them, not only as the mere mudsills of civilization, but as criminals because of their poverty." Another regarded it as "a proclamation of justice in behalf of the poor outcasts" who are the victims "of our damnable system of misgovernment." It then observed: "Whatever may be the opinions of the plutocrats, the aristocrats and all the other rats," the people "will bless you for this brave word." Recognizing its radical character, a Newton,

Kansas, editor warned Lewelling that "the subsidized Press will go after you, and all the little 'me too' fellows will shout '*arnicky*.' " Still another, informing the governor that the groups who created tramps would be "the first to denounce" him, stated: "If this is anarchy, then I am an anarchist." A writer who styled himself "The Tramp Preacher" saw this "*nation of the unemployed*" as the basis for "the devouring revolution of retributive justice!" A Connecticut woman wrote Lewelling in the same vein: " I am almost hoping that somewhere the new nation may be actually started out of the unemployed this winter & grow to eat up the old nation." And a former Kansan, residing in California, noted simply: "These are certainly poor times to confine hungry men in bull-pens and on rock-piles, unless their families . . . be confined and fed with them." Finally, as with Debs, support came from the ranks of labor: Local 98, Knights of Labor, in Minneapolis congratulated him for his desire "not to punish Man, for a crime to wich the government has driven them, by its unjust class laws." A local of the International Association of Machinists in Brainerd, Minnesota, and "the different labor organizations of Cincinnati and Vicinity" expressed similar sentiments.[13]

On the severity of tramp statutes, a Denver police magistrate related to Lewelling: "I know of no laws which have been so universally abused and used as an engine of oppression against the unfortunate poor." This is true, a Texas lawyer named Andrew Jackson pointed out, because local officials "are paid fees in criminal cases only in case of conviction." Law thus becomes "an engine of oppression, startling in its operation," for "it has fostered a slave trade" through "the selling of honest and innocent men for the fees of officers." But these letters merely hint at what existence meant for the so-called "tramp": the utter destitution, the loss of dignity, the harassment born of being forced always to move on—with no resting place. This experience can only be recounted by one living through those days.[14]

R. L. Robinson, a cook steadily employed until the depression, told Lewelling of his wandering in search of work: "After arriving at Kewanee we went to the calaboose and explained our circumstances and ask permission to stay over night, to which the officer in charge readily consented." A place to sleep was found: "So after being searched we were placed in a cell there being no covering but simply an iron bench to lay upon but we were thankfull for even that and tried to sleep." Then the cycle began anew—interrogations, removal to another town, ceaseless shunting from jail to jail: "About one oclock we were comanded to get up and go into the office where we were subject to a cross-examanation as to where we had worked & after which we were told to get into the cell again." The writer continued, "And talking in a [tone] much worse than a man would talk to a dog he said we had come to town on the bridge and we would have to get out in the same manner the first thing in the morning." The letter closed on a pathetic note. What today is sound sociological insight was here the realization of one going under: "I think such treatment as that would soon make a criminal of me, and I really believe that many criminals are made in this manner." This was the social existence Populism knew and resisted, this the brutality of self-reliant men transformed into submissive, unthinking creatures—or criminals.[15]

Thus protest was urgent, or the meaning of resistance would be lost, acquiescence insured, and society never again challenged. Brutality therefore affected mind as well as body; for Populism society must stifle the very idea of social protest to pass safely through the coming crisis. Lester C. Hubbard, state chairman of the Illinois People's party, suggested this position when he noted that the people had "been drugged by these malign corporations," and that Illinois "now lies prostrate in narcotized slumber." Nor was this voluntary; corporate power has created a highly manipulative situation: "We shall have a distinct *caste* of the enormously rich. These men will be timorous as to the security of their vast holdings and utterly unscrupulous in their means of defense." Bayard Holmes, Chicago physician and later People's party mayoralty candidate of that city, was more direct. "Monopoly knows that it cannot control the markets of the people," he wrote Lloyd, "unless they also control the minds, and I believe we can look for a more and more aggressive policy on their part in this direction." Significantly, this policy might also produce unintentional consequences: "In fact, in their aggressiveness and fanaticism lies our greatest hope of safety. If tyrants will be moderate, the people will never rise against them." [16]

Lloyd himself viewed intellectual coercion in a still larger context; dominant groups actually initiate social protest, thereby guiding radicalism into safe channels: "The workingmen are turning desparately to politics for a remedy, not noticing that the most strenuous in urging that policy are the very class against whom they are struggling." Hence, protest becomes totally harmless: " 'The classes' will just as shrewdly and ruthlessly nullify the political, as they have already nullified, the industrial efforts of the 'masses' to better themselves." In fact, protest serves as a safety valve forestalling more basic changes; it keeps alive the fiction that society can still be challenged. "It is their serene consciousness of their ability to do this that makes all their newspapers and spokesmen so voluble in urging the workingmen to abandon the 'criminal folly of strikes,' and betake themselves to their sovereignty at the ballot-box."

Yet, Lloyd continued, this plan worked only because its ultimate foundation was sheer force: "In no event, will the workingmen and farmers be allowed, no matter what their majority, to take the control of the government." If necessary, violence would be manufactured as a pretext for enforcing submission; at all costs, control would not be surrendered. "If the people will not, out of their bovine peaceableness, do the acts of violence that would afford the pretext for the 'saviors of society' to keep possession, these latter will themselves commit the violence, and charge it upon the people." With the Pullman strike in mind, he observed, "They did this in Chicago, I verily believe. They have done it in many proceeding strikes. It is their winning card. Violence, Sedition they must have, of the people." Lloyd somberly added: "History rewrites itself in every great crisis." [17]

Thus, force underlay the intellectual quietude; militias and armories shaped opinion. Newspaper support for "the organization of military companies among the wealthy classes," observed a letter to one Nebraska paper, demonstrates that "a subsidized press is in league with the moneyed aristocracy to lull the people to sleep while the chains of slavery are being forged." Two years later the paper itself attacked a proposal for military training. The Lamont report, charged the *Alliance-Independent*, sought to inculcate the habit of obedience in youth. It was a reaction to "these times of increasing industrial war, foreshadowed by Homestead," times when "it is thought prudent to begin with the children and youth." The Topeka *Advocate*, as usual, was more direct; militias and armories had one function—to prevent social protest: "The companies and regiments organized to occupy these city bastiles and equipped with the latest improved instruments of death constitute a private army directly under the command of the capitalists of these cities, and ready, at their instance, to suppress any uprising of the common herd." Thus, "It would seem sufficiently clear to the unbiaesed mind from these facts that we are even now far on the road to the establishment of a military despotism in this country." [18]

And B. O. Flower of the *Arena*, in a letter to an Iowa Populist leader, stated: "If you could see how the armories are going up in the East, you would appreciate the fact that plutocracy is not only alarmed but is determined." "Here in Boston," he continued, "we have a large armory going up . . . for the crack Boston regiment and Boston cadets; and every dollar of money which it will cost . . . is being paid by private subscription." With protest suppressed at every turn, the lines were now tightening: "After the imprisonment of Coxey for stepping on the grass and the arrest of Fitzgerald for free speech in Philadelphia, and other outrages of recent occurrence, the people can see plainly what they have to expect." The tempo had noticeably quickened; the watershed was almost here.[19]

✤

CHAPTER THREE

THE FARMER
AND WORKING CLASS
DISCONTENT

Farmers felt at one with workers, not through an ideology of producer values but a conviction that both groups had been reduced to the same economic position. Success in the common struggle depended on mutual support; their futures were now intertwined. "The farmers and laborers," complained a letter to the *Alliance*, "are looked upon as a class but a little above the brutes; all we are fit for is to toil and support the whole business." Degradation, not simply wages and hours, was at issue; agrarians recognized, in the words of the *Alliance-Independent*, that labor opposed an economic system requiring "men in gangs, men 'known only by their number,' men wifeless and childless, men who will live in hovels and on offal." Thus, the paper continued, labor must be allowed to organize, for the isolated worker is helpless against the system. "In the condition of the labor market today, the laborer without an organization is at the mercy of an organized capital that knows no mercy." Nor would the creation of unions be easy: "Capital's combines have issued the edict that labor organizations must be destroyed. They have begun the war on them at Homestead, at Coeur Alene—where not?" The issue was the character of society itself; farmers and workers must combine. "Not in vain have the workers of town and country touched hands in fraternal greeting. At last they recognize their common interests." Or, as a paper read to a local Alliance meeting in Nebraska stated, "Thus we see organized capital arrayed against the producers . . . The irrepressible conflict between capital and labor is upon us." [1]

Lester C. Hubbard expressed the same view in a letter to Lloyd: "There is war in the land—between a Compact Plutocracy on one side—and the unorganized worker on the other. I think the need of the time is to establish the moral solidarity of the farmer and toiler societies." The *Alliance* also suggested the common interest based upon shared adversity: "The same forces which are to day depriving the workingman of a living for himself and family and making him a meek and humble slave, are at work upon the farmer." A Minnesota state Farmers' Alliance declaration of rights in 1886—its early date is all the more important—provides an even clearer statement: "The degradation and impoverishment of either class is a direct blow at the prosperity of the other." Further, "The natural enemies of both are the men who fasten themselves upon the producers to get something for nothing." And the *Farmers' Alliance and Nebraska Independent* similarly noted, "We know that the interests of rural and urban labor are the same and that their enemies are the private controllers of credit, commerce and land that others must use, those who by our present laws have power to collect from the workers, interest and unjust freights and rents." [2]

Agrarians had still another reason for supporting labor;

radicalism could only be made effective through united action. The *Farmers' Alliance* constantly urged this position. Basic changes would not be possible, a Cornell, Nebraska, letter warned in 1889, until the government was "brought under the control of the laboring classes." The paper itself characterized Nebraska in 1890 as "only one of the out-skirts in the line of battle" against monopoly. Noting several weeks later an unprecedented "uprising of the agricultural and wage-earning people of the country," it welcomed the trend as a necessary first step: "there must be a change and a bettering of the condition of the wage-earner and the producer." "The attempted seizure of the government by plutocrats and plutocracy," it insisted, "must be throttled, *shall be throttled,* by free American independents." And a letter from North Platte in 1891 captured the sense of common hardship affecting both groups. "The man hunting work," it began, "knows there is plenty of work to do. He sees there is no 'overproduction' to cause men to be idle. For if he sees the elevators and cribs full of corn in Illinois, at the same time he knows of the hungry stock and hungry people in the west." Nor did each hold the other responsible; society itself created misery in the midst of potential abundance: "And before when he saw the west overloaded with corn, which the people had to burn because they could get no coal, at the same time he knew of the thousands of tons of coal banked in Illinois; of 20,000 hungry and idle miners." With farmers and workers thus "getting poorer each year, and the monopolists and money changers waxing richer and richer," there is no alternative but a coalition of "every farmer, mechanic and laborer." [3]

With the Homestead strike in mind, a letter to the

Topeka *Advocate* expressed the need for a coalition even more strongly: "We condemn anarchy, but we detest the causes that produce it even more. These evils are all the legitimate children of the oppression of capital, and again the oppressor is the aggressor." Force, if anything, merely underscored the necessity. "We shall continue to hope for a peaceable solution of these differences, but we fear the haughty tyranny of capital will persist in its resort to war measures by the use of Pinkertons and militia beyond the point of endurance." [4]

Agrarians viewed even isolated strikes in larger terms. These disputes concerned not specific grievances but the very structure of society. For the *Farmers' Alliance*, the 1890 New York Central strike involved the principle of unions: "The right of labor to organize is attacked by the best organized capitalistic force of the country." Hence, strikes are justifiable: "Labor must fight its own battles, and fight them with the only weapon it has at hand." Unions are the only answer; isolated workers are "a multitude of atoms—mere individual men, necessary to the corporation certainly, but with no rights the corporation is bound to respect, or if bound nominally to respect their rights having power enough to practically ignore them." "And yet," the editorial reflected, "the atoms are the ones who produce the wealth." The *Alliance-Independent*, referring to Homestead, incisively noted: "All who look beneath the surface will see that the bloody battle fought at Homestead was a mere incident in the great conflict between labor and capital." The strike, it argued two weeks later, "is not so much over the scale of wages, as it is over the destruction or perpetuation" of the union. The principle of organization was crucial: "The laborers will resist this warfare with all their power. It is not a matter of mere sentiment with them. They realize that their only protection against the tyranny of capital lies in their union." The paper cautioned, "Once this is broken up, the capitalist will only have the individual laborers to deal with. He can then use the laborers to beat down their own wages through competition for employment." [5]

The *Advocate* regarded Homestead as a sign "of the general unrest that everywhere pervades society throughout the world." This strike had one goal, to resist the trend toward subsistence living for the worker: "The tendency of the times is to constantly lower the standard of wages paid to labor in order to constantly add to the accumulations of the non-producing classes. The strikes that occur from time to time are merely local protests against this general policy." The subsistence wage was related to one factor—surplus workers; industrial society created a surplus labor force "for the purpose, to displace organized labor, always at lower wages than have been formerly paid." Further, the policy was based on force; unions must be broken before it could succeed. Pinkertons, state and federal troops, "under the pretense of protection to vested rights, can always be relied upon to assist in the displacement and to see that it is accomplished to the satisfaction of the employers of labor." Mary E. Lease, best known of the Populist female campaigners, in a letter to the *Advocate* the next week, charged Carnegie with trying "to perpetuate a system of social cannibalism, and force, by the aid of Pinkerton cutthroats." Praising Kansas farmers for "sending provisions to the locked-out Homestead laborers," she then

warned, "the fight at Homestead is only the beginning
of the battle against organized labor." In fact, "What has
been there will be repeated in detail in every great plutocratic establishment now employing union labor in the
United States." Thus, Mrs. Lease closed, "In this fight
the labor forces in all departments must stand together." [6]

The president of a district Alliance in Kansas characterized the strike in these terms: "Capitalists are now
waging a war of extermination against labor organizations with a view of reducing the individual workers to
a state of abject servitude." And the Alliance of Mitchell
county, Kansas, resolved, in its offer to help "the union
laborers at Homestead, Pa., in their determined, just and
sacred efforts," that "we condemn our present industrial
system which subjects the laborer in the field, in the shop
or mine, to the merciless and soulless moneyed corporations as to what he is to receive for the products of his
labor. . ." For the farmer the Homestead striker was not
alone; each needed the other if "all who earn their daily
bread by the sweat of their brow" were to survive as
human beings.[7]

Agrarians also supported warmly the Coxey industrial
army; this march on Washington was the so-called tramp
crying out for justice. "The Coxey movement," Lewelling stated some five months after his proclamation, "is
a spontaneous uprising of the people. It is more than a
petition, it is an earnest and vigorous protest against the
injustice and tyranny of the age." He urged, "Here in
Kansas the people should hold public meetings to encourage the movement." The *Advocate* held that "all
reference to the causes which have produced" Coxeyites
is "studiously avoided." Instead, they are merely "con-

temptuously spoken of as cranks, tramps and vagabonds." The paper's own view was very different: "Men do not become tramps and vagabonds from choice." It then observed, in words similar to the personal account received by Lewelling: "When forced into idleness and compelled to take to the road in the fruitless effort to find employment it requires but a short time to make a vagabond of the man who under other and more favorable circumstances would be numbered among our best citizens." Hence, society emphatically must be blamed for the industrial army. "The causes which force people into idleness are therefore responsible, not only for this Coxey movement, but for nearly all the lawlessness and crime of the country, as well." [8]

Two weeks later the *Advocate* remarked, in justifying the march on Washington, that the unemployed have as much right to "demand justice at the hands of congress as bankers, railroad magnates and corporation attorneys have to go and lobby for measures by which to plunder the public." Yet, not all are accorded the same reception in Washington. The *Advocate* noted in the next issue the results of a workers' demonstration against the Wilson tariff: "Manufacturers engaged in the protected industries in Eastern cities rig out a lot of their employes in guady raiment and send them up to the national capital in palace cars." The paper then queried, "Were these men headed off by the police and the national guard and forbidden to enter the sacred precincts of the capital?" "No," it replied, "they were met by a brass band and nothing was too good for them." Nine months later, closing its discussion of industrial armies, the *Advocate* held that people, "reduced to helpless want by the cruel conditions of our glorious social and industrial system, are thus shuffled about from place to place day after day —told to move on when they have no place on earth to go to"—here plaintively adding, "as though they were not recognized as human beings." The paper concluded simply, "Where, in God's name, are these people to go, and what are they to do?" [9]

Local Alliances in Nebraska also wondered what would become of these people. "We view with just alarm," stated a resolution from the Oak Valley Alliance of Lancaster county, "the excited condition of our people, over the Common-Weal army now marching to Washington." This march is absolutely justified: "We believe it is a right and dutie of these men at this time to go to Washington the capitol of our common country, the Congress of the U.S. being now in session, and there p[r]esent a living petition of their poverty and suffering." Thus, the cause of labor must be supported: "While we desire peace and an honorable adjustment of the differance's that so widely seperate labor and capital, still bleving the demands of labor to be just, we will not receed one attom from these demands." Nor were agrarians frightened by the charge of anarchy; this movement, asserted the Burt county Alliance, was "filled by honest laborers & loyal american citizens who are peaceably striving to petition congress in the interests of the unemployed, & laboring people generally." Hence, it continued, we "warmly sympathize with Gen. Coxey & his followers," and "severely cirtisise the actions toward them by the authorities at Washington." It added, referring to Populists in Congress who defended Coxey, we "warmly commend our representatives in congress for their faithful efforts in behalf of the producing classes of our country." [10]

Letters to the Nebraska Alliance state secretary reflect an even more grass-roots view of industrial armies. A member of the Sheridan county Alliance, having in mind the Washington episode, invited her to a picnic where "no one Will be *arested* For Steping on the Grass or Caring *Banners*." A letter from Sacramento, Nebraska, informed her, "Coxey and Kelley have a great many sympathizers here." And one from Cambridge, Nebraska, reported, "We are all stirred up with the report of Coxey and the treatment and arrest of his commanders The brutal treatment of men, women, and children by the hireling police." And in Osceola, Nebraska, from four to six thousand people attended a picnic in Coxey's honor. "Early in the morning," according to a local paper, "strings of teams loaded with men, women and children, all anxious to see and hear Coxey, began arriving at the grove, and until after noon there was a continuous stream of people arriving." In fact, "the grove was filled to overflowing with people and all avalable space for hitching teams within a half mile of the grounds was occupied." [11]

Senator Allen of Nebraska, among the more conservative Populists, defended industrial armies on the Senate floor: "The conditions of the country are ripe to produce movements of this kind," yet Congress passively listens "without any attempt being made to redress their wrongs." Ten days later, in an article for the New York *Morning Journal*, Allen became more militant: "This country is most hopelessly in the grasp of the money power. Heroic efforts must be employed to change this condition of affairs." The Coxeyite movement was precisely such an effort: "If Mr. Coxey and his followers are able to bring about, or . . . hasten this desirable period, their mission will have been performed successfully." A question posed by the Lincoln *Wealth Makers* best summarizes these views: "Have not peaceful American citizens a right to petition congress in person?" Its answer was followed by an even more pressing question. "It is stupid or cruel to tell these men, these destitute starving millions, that they must right their wrongs at the ballot box. What are men sent to congress and to the White House for but to make laws to protect the weak, the poor, the preyed upon?" "Every monopolist in the land," it hoped, would be compelled daily to look at "a section of the poorest of our people who labor without gain that their oppressors may gain without labor, and who in the stagnation period of each usury cycle are not allowed to work at any price." Even the dissenting voice, national chairman Herman E. Taubeneck of Illinois, indicated by his very criticism that Populism strongly endorsed the Coxey movement. He wrote Donnelly in March 1894, "We can not in any way identify our party with this movement." More alarmed several weeks later, he added: "Some are apprehending that danger confronts us on this question." [12]

The Pullman strike provided yet another rallying point for farmers and workers. Here Populism began winning over Eugene V. Debs and the American Railway Union. Governor Davis Waite of Colorado told a Populist rally, "This strike can never succeed because the entire armed forces of the United States are against the success of the laboring man." In a word, "the United

States government is using all its military power to build up monopoly." And Annie Diggs, like Mrs. Lease a fiery orator from Kansas, asked the same rally, "Who is helping the A.R.U. and the laboring men but the Populist party?" Calling for a strike fund, she stated: "There are a great many people here who would be willing to help the men who have been shut out of employment." Lewelling's firm position on Pullman was praised by the Argentine, Kansas, local of the union as "manly and honorable sentiments" which "has depreciated the Methods and Utterances of Federal Officers and others in dealing with the Labor Question and has shown and expressed a feeling of fraternal interest toward the Honorable efforts of Laboring Men to better their Condition." The trades assembly of Kansas City, Kansas, also commended Lewelling for "his recent letter referring to the Pullman boycott, and . . . for the courage displayed in expressing himself in favor of organized labor and against corporations." [13]

On the agrarian side, a letter to the governor from Larned, Kansas, maintained: "Unquestionably, nearly, if not quite, all Alliance people are in fullest sympathy with these striking men." "The present," it continued, "is an opportune moment to take such a[c]tion as may be taken in order to render assistance in a struggle that bids fair to be fought to the bitter end on both sides." And a correspondent in White City, Kansas, wrote, "God Bless you 'for the stand you have taken Regarding the Pullman Co.' Stand firm and you will find that most of us Pops, are right in line." Finally, the People's party central committee of Kansas City endorsed the governor's stand in these terms: "We sympathize with the

American Railway Union in its fight with the Pullman monopoly and that we approve of the attitude of Governor Lewelling as shown by an interview published in to-days Kansas City papers." [14]

Significantly, the strike intensified the Populist discussion on the railroad question itself—an issue already founded on a long history of grievances. Here belief in government ownership and support for labor converge. For the Lincoln *Wealth Makers* the strike was "forcing upon the attention of the country the necessity of taking out of private, selfish hands the railroads upon which all commerce and production now so largely depend." Thus, "The railroad question is looming up as one of gigantic proportions, and one that must be dealt with without delay." In one sense, then, the strike was fortunate; it sharpened the issue. "We are not sorry that the pressure of events, the conflict of mighty organized forces, is awakening the people of the entire country to think and take action." The alternative was simple: "We must run the railroads or permit them to decree and collect tribute of us all and carry on war against their employes." And the paper's recommendation was emphatic: "Public ownership of the public highways and means of transportation is no longer a question of economy, but it is forced upon [us] as a necessity." There was also a more immediate issue; labor's right to organize was at stake: Corporations "*are fighting for the preservation of their power to dictate all terms to their employes.*" Three weeks later the *Wealth Makers* raised what it believed was the central meaning of Pullman: "Combined labor must be crushed by the federal troops and by the courts." [15]

The Topeka *Advocate* likewise believed the strike "has taught lessons that nothing else could have taught." These included "the absolute necessity of government ownership and operation of railroads" and labor's recognition that "the republican and democratic parties are on the side of capital." Labor should now realize that its "only political friends in this country to-day are the Populists." But more important for this paper was the problem of violence. These acts in the strike, it insisted, were "deliberately created by the companies and by the deputies and the military sent ostensibly to preserve the peace, in order to manufacture sentiment against the strikers." Violence, it stated in the next issue, was "at once attributed to the strikers in order to create prejudice against them." This would, as Lloyd also noted, "afford a pretext for police and military interference." "In any difference between capital and labor," the paper continued, "courts and all the civil and military authorities are at the service of organized capital." The *Advocate* bitterly closed, "Labor has no right that capital or its allies are bound to respect." And in connection with the Debs trial two months later, it reaffirmed this view: "Put a corporation upon one side and a poor man upon the other and the courts will see to it that there is sufficient latitude to the law to satisfy the utmost demand of the corporation." [16]

John Davis, a Populist congressman from Kansas, regarded Pullman as one incident in the developing pattern of coercion: "We see rising up in the near future a military despotism seeking excuses for its own creation and growth." "Every 'march on Washington,' every labor strike, and every destruction of mines, bridges and railroads," Davis was convinced, "is but a further excuse for the plutocrats to increase and use without restraint the military power." [17]

For Populism, then, the defeat at Pullman was a testimony to the coercive features of industrial America. Six months later, when the smoke had cleared, the *Advocate* observed that the question of the legality of using troops was insignificant compared with "what the consequences will be to the liberties of the American people." It wondered, "Are we ready for the recognition of an imperial government?" Lewelling, delivering his annual message the week before, had also given serious thought to coercion. Kansas coal operators, he charged, deliberately sought to nullify a state law on screening coal in order "to provoke the miners to strike." The result was the creation of a state within the state, one dictating its own policies: "Having accomplished this purpose, the operators of Cherokee and Crawford counties proceeded to erect private forts, garrisoned with conscienceless mobs armed with Winchester rifles, intended to commit murder in resisting mere trespasses upon lands." The governor, however, was determined "to refuse military aid to corporations engaged in an armed revolt against the law of the state." In a word, corporate power would not rule Kansas: "The only forts on Kansas soil should be those erected by the constituted authorities of the state or of the general government." [18]

Agrarian support extended beyond Homestead, Pullman, and the Capitol lawn; the less sensational accounts, such as the treatment of Debs in the Nebraska press, provide a more accurate picture of the sentiment toward labor. The *Alliance-Independent*, six months before

Pullman, observed that Debs "is not only leading the railway employes to organize for mutual assistance and resistance to tyranny, but he is with great ability educating them to vote intelligently and independently." Its own response was, "In behalf of our people in Nebraska we reach out earnest hands of brotherhood to those whose co-operative and educational lines of labor converge and agree with ours. The interests of the producing classes are one and indivisible." The Populist paper in Broken Bow stated after the strike that "Debs is in jail but his spirit is entering into the bosoms of millions of patriotic defenders of liberty." Three months later, discussing the "grand reception" which awaits him upon leaving jail, it added: "Debs stands higher today in the hearts of the masses than any labor leader in America. All friends of humanity and justice delight to do him honor." The Wahoo paper charged that "the malicious imprisonment of Eugene V. Debbs" signified "a new phase of things." The judicial system opposed rather than protected the individual: "We had supposed the courts were for the protection of the citizens, but now the citizens has to be protected from the courts?" By May 1896 it endorsed Debs as the People's party candidate; he would have "the strongest following to start on of any candidate of any party in the field." And the O'Neill paper linked him with Senator Allen as "the strongest combination that the People's Party could nominate." Thus, they "would harmonize and bring together more struggling humanity than any two prominent men known to the reform movement today." [19]

Agrarian hostility to the Pinkerton is yet another sign of its over-all position on labor. The *Farmers' Alliance* referred to the use of Pinkertons in the 1890 New York Central strike in these terms: "The most notable and alarming feature of all the business is the indifference of all local authorities to the glaring violation of law and infringement of all sound constitutional principles involved in the employment of this force; or worse, the subserviency of the authorities to the corporations which employ it." The people cannot long tolerate " the arbitrary and despotic sway of an overgrown corporate power," which directs "the great plain people" not to organize while it is "itself organizing, and which arrogates to itself all dominion and function which belongs to the people." [20]

The *Advocate* was less sparing; Pinkertons were "a lawless band of mercenaries subject to hire of millionaire corporations." Their function was "to murder troublesome employes who conceive the idea that they are entitled to the common rights of American freemen." The *Advocate's* response to the Brooklyn railroad strike of 1895 was even more critical: "These Pinkerton thugs and hired assassins are always at the service of arrogant corporations. They constitute a private army under the command of neither state or national authority, but always at the service of capital in its every contest with labor." Indignantly, the paper asked, "Do the people of this country see no danger from a force of this character?" Further, Pinkertons helped create, and were themselves recruited from, a surplus labor force: "It is to the interest of these corporate employers of labor that there shall always be an army of idle men in the country upon the very verge of starvation who may be relied upon to take the places of strikers in all difficulties of this kind."

Hence, Pinkertons are more than scabs; they stampede the unemployed, pit worker against worker, and thereby prevent the very formation of unions. "Without such an idle force, no corporation could hope to succeed against any labor strike." The ranks of surplus labor must be swelled with Pinkertons present to insure that many compete for one place—and on the employer's terms: "A strike occurring with no such force in reserve would simply mean a recognition of the rights of labor, or a stoppage of business, and hence the employers of labor encourage the conditions that produce idleness as a means of security to their own arbitrary designs." As for the strike itself, the *Advocate* commented: "No matter if men are required to work fourteen or sixteen hours per day at starvation wages, if they strike nothing is heard of these abuses, but great stress is laid upon the duty of government to protect 'the rights of the people' against interference by strikers." Yet, " 'the rights of the people' are always spoken as though the strikers themselves were no part of the people, and as though they have no rights that are to be considered." [21]

Militias fared little better in Populist hands. The Wahoo, Nebraska, paper chided McKinley in 1896 for his plea to restore 1892 conditions: "Has he forgotten the butcheries and attrocities at Coer de Alene and in Tennessee mines, where malitia and U.S. troops murdered in cold blood hundreds of suffering laborers under the dictates of Wall Street?" The Broken Bow paper happily quoted a colonel in the Nebraska militia upon his resignation: "The state soldiery throughout the Union has been organized always at the behest, and often at the dictation, of corporate capital, which asks that the state plunge its bayonets into the breast of organized labor in order to enforce compliance with organized capital's demands." The paper then added on its own account: "It is dawning upon conscientious militiamen that they are being made tools of to overawe and browbeat naturally peaceful citizens in the interest of the selfish class." And Lewelling, well before his 1895 message, complained to a Topeka editor that private armies were being created through "the aggression of the courts." Once permit corporations "to employ armed men to protect their property," he warned, "the number of men so employed may be unlimited and the great corporations may thus maintain a standing army which becomes a menace to the peace and dignity of the state." [22]

The agrarian view was expressed in other realms as well. A letter from Madison, Kansas, wanted the eradication of slums inserted into the 1892 St. Louis platform: "We cannot rest until such environments are completely wiped out, and every child born into the world has a chance to grow heavenward in body mind & heart." On the Pennsylvania mining riots of 1894, the *Advocate* held that most newspapers, "so loud in their denunciations of the 'anarchistic' demonstrations of laboring men, are as silent as the tomb concerning the avarice and greed and systematic plunder which have driven these men to desperation, and thereby provoked the violent acts which are so severly condemned." Significantly, its position on Governor Altgeld's pardon of those involved at Haymarket was also at variance with the bulk of public opinion: "We know that the trial in question and the punishment inflicted upon those men was a most deadly blow to human liberty in America." Not content with this indictment, it added, "They were persecuted by organized capital because they were prominent advocates of the rights of labor, and not because they were guilty of any act of violence." [23]

Clearly, the agrarian attitude toward labor meant more than sympathy and nostalgia; it meant economic necessity, a farmer-labor coalition to challenge industrial America. Yet, Populism never emerged in this light; it was not a genuine farmer-labor movement. A tentative conclusion concerning the reason for this failure, springing directly from the evidence, can now be stated: That agrarians wanted the coalition is unquestioned; hence, the conservative, retarding influence lay elsewhere— *with labor*.

The *Advocate*, for example, was acutely aware that agrarians were more radical than the working class as a whole. This position was developed in the course of its criticism of an Illinois supreme court decision invalidating the forty-eight hour week for women in factories: "Everyone knows that the right of contract means the right of capital in all cases to impose any conditions it may desire upon labor, simply because labor, unprotected, is powerless to reject the provisions of such contract, whatever they may be." When there is surplus labor, freedom of contract is a farce. "In the present state of society, with a limited market for labor and thousands of idle men and women anxiously seeking opportunity to earn bread, there is no such thing as freedom of contract in the ranks of labor, and it is worse than nonsense to talk about it." But labor does nothing; it acquiesces, even blindly supports this state of affairs.

Here the *Advocate* was bitter: "In this, as in other things, however, labor is getting what it has been voting for, and it has no right to squeal." Three months later, discussing technological unemployment, it leveled the same charge: "The worst feature of the situation is that the very fool workingmen who are deprived of the means of subsistence will continue to vote for the perpetuation of the system which is constantly adding to the number of unemployed just as often as they get a chance." It added, "Vote her straight, boys; you may get enough of it in the course of time." [24]

Ethelbert Stewart, a sympathetic and experienced student of labor, argued the point more persuasively. Writing Lloyd that they were "good enough friends to be able to scold each other," Stewart chided him for expressing doubts "about the farmers last night." Citing Ohio, Stewart noted that "the farmers met and demanded government ownership of railroads, then they invited the Miners Convention to sit with them." And when the miners called for "state or government ownership of coal mines," he continued, "the farmers voted for it in convention and will vote for it this fall." Neither farmers nor workers have a monopoly on radicalism; segments of each remain outside Populism: "Not all farmers, nor will all the union men in Chicago, to say nothing of all laboring men, all union men in Chicago will not vote the People's ticket." Simply, "There are farmers, and farmers; the rich farmer who rents out all his farm but the homestead '40,' is in sympathy with capitalism; but if the vote could be put to the farmers today on governmental ownership of railroads it would carry two to one." Significantly, Stewart remarked: "I am not sure it would in the cities." That agrarians were split should not therefore obscure the radical views of the poorer farmers. And while agrarian radicalism was still confined to specific issues, this does not mean that farmers were opposed to broader programs. The potential was present; only awareness was lacking: "As to collective ownership of means of production the farmer has never thought about it much; but he has thought of railroads, and he is not a barbarian." [25]

Historians perhaps have erred, then, in regarding agrarians as the stumbling block in a farmer-labor movement. The farmer's willingness was too manifest to be ignored. As early as 1891, for example, the minutes of the Gove county, Kansas, Alliance reveal that agrarians identified themselves with the working class. As "residents of the Drouth Stricken regions of western Kans." who "are laboring under great Finacial embarrasment," this group now responded to the call "made for representation from the various labor Organizations of the U.S. to meet in Cincinnatti, May 19th 1891." The preamble read, "We are in sympathy with said movement, believing that the time has come for the laboring classes to Demand their rights by united Political action Having disolved our old Political affiliations, we desire to act in harmony with all other labor organizations for the attainment of our just rights." "Therefore Resolve," it went on, "that we (the Gove Co Union) unanimously favor the organization of new National Reform party, and pledge our selves to its support." This undoubtedly was the raw material for a farmer-labor movement. [26]

Yet, there is a tendency instead to accept at face value labor's own explanation for the failure—Samuel Gompers' dictum in the July 1892 *North American Review* that an alliance was undesirable because agrarians were "*employing* farmers." Surely, the evidence suggests the opposite; Gompers opposed agrarians for being too radical, and not too conservative. Dissension at the 1894 American Federation of Labor convention also bears this out. Rank-and-file opposition to the Gompers stand on both independent political action and the famous plank 10 indicates that he met with hostility on questions affecting not only Populism but radicalism as a whole. Further, the fact that approximately three hundred labor candidates entered the 1894 campaign against his express policy, many of these as Populists, points to Gompers as speaking more for a conservative labor elite. Finally, his refusal to support Bryan in 1896 merely underscores his stance throughout the period, a position prompting one member of his own executive board to retort: "To me it is indeed strange how a man can believe in a question as an economic demand and be opposed to the same principle as soon as it becomes a political question." These are hard facts on Gompers and his sophistry; indeed, his statement on Populism was not made with clean hands.[27]

Lloyd saw clearly in 1894 that the Federation shaped the future of Populism. Having tapped the maximum radical support in that campaign, Populism now confronted its destiny: With help, it could expand into a farmer-labor movement; otherwise, it most certainly would slide backward. In effect, as Lloyd already had sensed, the Federation played a crucial *negative* role. While its weight was essential to a stronger third party, its failure to act guaranteed the ultimate downfall of Populism.

This is why Lloyd wrote Gompers on bended knee that summer, "What is needed in my view is a delegate assembly of all the reform elements to give immediate direction and concentration to the acts of the people in the coming election." Populism had fought alone; it could no longer do so: "Such a convention could make terms for the workingmen with the People's Party and the Socialist Labor Party and the Single Taxers that would be equal to the fruits of ten years of agitation." And Populism should be the core of this movement: "If such a convention gave the word as I think it would and as I think it ought to do—*for this moment*—that all the voters of discontent should unite on the candidates of the People's Party, we would revolutionize the politics of this country." Anticipating the refusal of Gompers, Lloyd then catered to his vanity: "The time has come for the leaders to lead. No man in history has had a greater opportunity for usefulness and glory than now begs you to embrace it. The people are scattered, distracted, leaderless, waiting for just such guidance." Populism, indeed radicalism itself, was poised at the threshold; support must come now: "And the opportunity will not recur." Labor therefore had life-and-death power over Populism. "If not taken now the reins will pass to other hands or what is more likely, no reins will be able to control the people." True, external factors— an unresponsive two-party system, intimidation and economic coercion—helped prevent the spread of Populism. Insofar as purely internal factors counted, however, the fault lay not with agrarians but with labor, particularly its leadership. That Debs was a Populist gave the lie to the Gompers argument; the Federation, through looking the other way, killed the farmer-labor movement. At least, so thought a now stranded Populism.[28]

Nor were farmer-labor ties nonexistent on the local level; in fact, their prevalence serves to indict national labor leaders even more. Minnesota serves as an excellent illustration. The president of the Duluth Municipal Reform Association wrote Edwin Atwood in 1890: "We will support the farmers in the coming campaign no matter who the nominees are, if straight Independence is meant." This policy would not be easy; attempts were constantly being made to divide farmers and workers. "You can feel assured that our efforts will be directed towards harmonizing all reform elements and squelching out any side show that may be introduced to lead the farmers and laborers off the track." A letter to Ignatius Donnelly also warned against this danger: "So long as these two armies can be kept at swords points monopoly is secure." Specifically, "with the corporation press carrying lies from one side to the other, the mechanics and farmers are like prisoners lashing each other for the pleasure of a third party." It buoyantly closed: "When the flag of truce has been raised long enough to come to an understanding, they will join forces and make for the common enemy, who, when he sees the combination, will follow the example of Davy Crockett's coon and come down without delay." And a state representative also regarded the question of divisive tactics as an especial bane of the coalition: "Every posseble means has been used to belittle the work of the Alliance Members, and also to . . . get up a quarrel between the Alliance and Laboring Men." [29]

The seeds for a coalition can be seen in perfect microcosm from an exchange in the *Representative*. George W. Morey, secretary of the state Federation of Labor, wrote Donnelly that his organization "desires the closest possible affiliation with the Farmer's Alliance"

and invites them "to send delegates to our meeting."
Here he reasoned, "Our interests are certainly along the
same lines, and . . . we are inclined to favor similar
methods." Donnelly replied that the Alliance "clearly
recognizes the fact that one great interest binds together
all who labor to produce the real wealth of the world."
Significantly, he explained, "The farmers fully under-
stand that they must look for a market for the produc-
tions of their fields not to the few thousand millionaires,
but to the vast army of . . . men who labor in the cities,
towns and villages." In sum, "Their interests are therefore our interests, and their enemies our enemies." Three
months later the *Representative*, which was Donnelly's
paper, attacked labor leaders who tried "to prevent the
working people from acting with the People's Party,
under a hundred different cunning practices." It then
urged workers not only to "move into the People's party
as a body," but to "regard every man who advises otherwise as the corrupt tool of Plutocracy." It closed with
this perhaps timeless observation: "Leadership is a mar-
ketable commodity now-a-days, and the enemy are
ready to buy it." [30]

Even Republicans were becoming restive; one noted
in 1891 that "thair are maney Republicans are talking
Strong on this fall election turning over to the Farmers
alience and the Labour ticket." This threatened, he
feared, to be a tidal wave: "The Faremers alience &
union Labour are talking Strong of uniting together.
also maney off our Repubelicans that voted at our last
Presidancel alection that wont vote with us a gaine."
But his fear was premature; the dike held.[31]

✤

CHAPTER FOUR

PHILOSOPHIC
DIGRESSION

Populism was certainly not Marxism; its vision of America was not socialized production and the collective farm. Yet, comparing the two, one finds such remarkable similarities as to suggest further proof that Populism was radical. For each, industrial capitalism meant alienated man—man divorced from himself, his product, and humanity. The *Farmers' Alliance* and Marx's *Economic and Philosophic Manuscripts* point up these same aspects of alienation. "The materialism of to-day," stated the *Farmers' Alliance*, "does all the time seggregate human lives." The issue is more than physical hardship: Man "is brutalized both morally and physically" so that the "divine spark" becomes "torpid in his soul." This dichotomized person also appears in Marx: "The worker . . . only feels himself outside his work, and in his work feels outside himself." Thus "what is animal becomes human and what is human becomes animal." On man's relation to his product, the *Farmers' Alliance* was concerned not with the sense of workmanship but with an exploitative productive system: "He knows that it is greed that enforces the material labor that is crushing him down." Further, the economy is an opposing force which makes the worker's position that "of a machine to its director." For Marx, "The *alienation* of the worker in his product means not only that his labour becomes an object, an *external* existence, but that it exists *outside* him, independently, as something alien to him, and that it becomes a power on its own confronting him." And the Populist paper saw man separated from his fellow men in these terms: "The tendency of the competitive system is to antagonize and disassociate men." The bonds of humanity are broken; man is in "a state of war." Marx likewise held that man is turned from "the *life of the species* into a means of individual life." Capitalism therefore "is the *estrangement of man* from *man.*" Nor was the similarity confined to a critique of the problem. The *Farmers' Alliance,* while not calling for the abolition of private property, did pose some leading questions: "How is he to have more time and more energy to develop his faculties except by lessening his hours of labor and increasing his wages? Can this be done under the present system?" Its reply clearly suggests the potential for a radical solution, one perhaps awaiting greater awareness or harder times: "There *must* be a better one." [1]

The second area of convergence deals with the creation of tramps and vagabonds: Lewelling's "Tramp Circular" and Marx on original accumulation in *Capital* see this as a central feature of capitalist development. Taking enclosures in Elizabethan England as the type-form, each finds men uprooted from a position of independence, forced as tramps to wander in search of work, and kept in a dependent condition through legal means. "In the reign of Elizabeth," Lewelling began, "the highways were filled with the throngs of the unemployed poor, who were made to 'move on,' and were sometimes brutally whipped, sometimes summarily hanged, as 'sturdy vagrants' or 'incorrigible vagabonds.' " Marx agreed; the unemployed "were turned *en masse* into beggars, robbers, vagabonds, partly from inclination, in most cases from stress of circumstances." Even his words were similar: "Hence at the end of the 15th and during the whole of the 16th century, throughout Western Europe a bloody legislation against vagabondage . . . Legislation treated them as 'voluntary' criminals, and assumed that it depended on their goodwill to go on working under the old conditions that no longer existed." Lewelling in turn denied that the unemployed were at fault; it was ridiculous to assume that anyone "being able bodied and willing to work can always find work to do." Further, both maintained that the change was monumental; man had become totally transformed. For Lewelling this "rendered more and more human beings superfluous," while for Marx it separated "the labourers from all property in the means by which they can realise their labour." Hence, it was "the historical process of divorcing the producer from the means of production." Yet, the remedies differed markedly, Lewelling contending only that poverty should "cease to be a crime." [2]

Nor does the resemblance end here; each treated ideology as a reflection of dominant group interests. For Populism the success myth was a fraud: "No effort of the people . . . could have averted these results." Hence, "While the cause exists the evils *must* and *will* remain." Social Darwinism was no better; it meant "not the survival of the fittest, but the survival of the strongest." And laissez faire brought about "the plutocracy of today," where "the corporation has absorbed the community." These ideologies, by denying social protest, sought to preserve the status quo; they could not be taken at face value. Thus, Populism expressed in practice what Marx observed in the *German Ideology*: "The ideas of the ruling class are in every epoch the ruling ideas." Even basic values had become perverted by current ideologies; freedom was now a mere shibboleth. Populism insisted that freedom could not be meaningful unless founded upon "*industrial* freedom, without which there can be no political freedom." Marx in *Capital* also regarded freedom as a fiction; in its present guise freedom was the right of a man to "dispose of his labour-power as his own commodity." A positive statement was therefore needed, one piercing through ideological subterfuges: For Populism individuality could only mean "the divinity of humanity," and freedom, human existence "devoted to rest, to mental culture, to social intercourse and recreation." Marx held up the same standard for judging freedom—the multi-faceted man who would be able "to hunt in the morning, fish in the afternoon, rear cattle in the evening, criticize after dinner . . . without ever becoming hunter, fisherman, shepherd or critic." [3]

Yet, Populism and Marxism differed on ideology in a notable respect: Marx sought the relation between ideological and material factors in society, delineating the role of capitalism, division of labor, and commodity fetishism in the rise of ideology. For Populism this was unknown territory. Lloyd spoke instead of manipulation: Dominant groups were "the most strenuous in urging" workers to protest, for the economic power of these groups insured their political dominance as well. While

Marx agreed with this on two counts—the primacy of economic over political factors, and the superficiality of reform politics—he studiously avoided the treatment of manipulation for its own sake. Even the famous statement on religion as "the opium of the people," in Marx's *A Criticism of the Hegelian Philosophy of Right*, was a complicated analysis of ideology, not a simplistic variation of conspiracy theory. "Man makes religion, religion does not make man. Religion indeed is man's self-consciousness and self-estimation while he has not found his feet in the universe. But Man is no abstract being, squatting outside the world. Man is the world of men, the State, society." Thus, "This State, this society produces religion, which is an inverted world. Religion is the general theory of this world, its encyclopaedic compendium, its logic in popular form. . ." In a word, Populism described the results of ideology, and Marx its causation. Still, Lloyd too rejected conspiracy theory: Personal intentions are irrelevant, for "the main point is the simple issue of monopoly." [4]

But the greatest affinity between Populism and Marxism lies in still a fourth area. Each pointed to the same economic features as defining capitalism. On the concentration of wealth, Populism held that capitalism transformed "the common property of all" into "the monopoly of the few." Hence, "the present cruelly unjust system" was "fast working the hopeless pauperization and degradation of the toiling masses." The "people have produced but they possess not," for now "the means of subsistence are monopolized." In sum, "more are reduced to dependence than rise to independence." Throughout volume one, part seven, of *Capital*, Marx noted the accumulation of wealth coupled with "the mass of misery, oppression, slavery," and other forms of hardship. More succinctly, he stated in *Capital:* "Accumulation of capital is, therefore, increase of the proletariat." For Populism labor became "merely a commodity" in this system, no more than "sponges to be squeezed and rats to be shot." Marx also regarded labor in this light; man was known by "this peculiar commodity, labour-power." Further, capitalism produced cyclical fluctuations: It drives down wages to the subsistence level, affirmed Populism, for "the workers are in constant want." And it "destroys the commercial equilibrium, makes the seller unable to buy back as much labor value as he sold, and so leads to glutted markets." Populism therefore offered an underconsumption theory for economic crisis, a view Marx maintained in volume three of *Capital:* "The last cause of all real crises always remains the poverty and restricted consumption of the masses" as compared to the development of productive forces "in such a way that only the absolute power of consumption of the entire society would be their limit." [5]

Yet, an important difference in scope emerges here: Marxism, unlike Populism, analyzed business cycles through the falling tendency of the rate of profit. Still, the difference is not as great as it seems. While Populism had no conception of rates of profit, its emphasis on underconsumption raises an interesting possibility. If Populism and Marxism did in fact agree on other essential points in economics, perhaps underconsumption is more central to the latter than is generally recognized. One economist argues precisely this—working, of course, from Marx, and not Populism: "Marx was giving advance notice of a line of reasoning which, if he had lived to complete his work, would have been of primary importance." It could not be otherwise—for Populism *or* Marxism. The basic social and economic fact in each is the surplus worker, one who by definition cannot adequately consume the products of society.[6]

For Populism capitalism depended upon the surplus worker: "The army of destitute unemployed is the source of its power." Hence, "It is in the interest of the capitalist class to have as many men as possible out of work and seeking it in order to keep and force wages down by making competition fierce." And the mechanism insuring this is "labor-saving machinery," from which "the capitalist has been the chief beneficiary." Since there was a "monopoly of machinery and other means of production and distribution," technological improvements could be specifically "used to displace labor." The fault lay with capitalism; under "a proper use of the instrumentalities of modern production and distribution" labor would not be cast down into poverty. The unemployed were thus "the natural product of a false and vicious system." Marx likewise focused in *Capital* on surplus labor and the role of technology: "Relative surplus-population is therefore the pivot upon which the law of demand and supply of labour works." Here machinery is crucial in displacing the worker, whether in the "form of the repulsion of labourers already employed, or the less evident but not less real form of the more difficult absorption of the additional labouring population through the usual channels." Marx concluded, "this surplus population becomes . . . the lever of capitalistic accumulation, nay, a condition of existence of the capitalist mode of production." This reliance upon the surplus worker suggests, then, the strong place of underconsumption in Marx. Nor did his view of machinery differ from that of Populism. He observed in the *Manifesto*, "The bourgeoise cannot exist without constantly revolutionising the instruments of production," and added in *Capital*, the bourgeois must "keep constantly extending his capital, in order to preserve it." Increased surplus labor therefore promotes surplus value; and capital accumulation merely renews the process, making possible "revolutions in the technical composition of capital, which . . . thereby reduce the relative demand for labor." [7]

Finally, each believed that capitalism developed through a dialectical process. Populism saw the tramp not only as "a natural product" but a basic trend of society: "The tendency of the times is to force the masses into a propertyless condition." The result is "a pivotal or turning point" in which "every element for good or *evil* is *developed to a* ripened maturity of forces." Since dominant groups "will NEVER consent" to fundamental reform, the crisis is fast approaching: "Without a complete eradication of this system the people cannot for once hope for relief of a permanent character." But Marx went further, a fact suggesting again that Populism and Marxism were concerned with different levels of the problem. While each might agree on the opening sentence of the *Manifesto*, class struggle was only the surface of dialectics for Marx. Hence, one does not find the Populist equivalent for Marx's preface to *A Contribution to the Critique of Political Economy:* "At a certain stage of their development, the material productive forces of society come in conflict with the existing relations of production. . ." Yet, the problem for each was still class struggle.[8]

This raises an interesting point on Populism itself: Although Populist statements on ruling groups and class struggle may appear dramatic, they are by no means an indication of irrationality. Not only do these notions logically follow from the total Populist critique; they also coincide with economic reality. It is therefore useful to recall, before discussing Populist thought as mere rhetoric, the classic study of George K. Holmes in 1893: Three-hundredths of one percent owned twenty percent of the national wealth, nine percent owned seventy-one percent, and the bottom fifty-two percent owned five percent. Holmes concluded, "4,047 families possess about seven-tenths as much as do 11,593,887 families." With this in mind, the Populist concern over class should not appear unreasonable.[9]

In any case, class struggle *was* in the air—and in the Populist press. In Nebraska alone, the Columbus paper charged, corporations "crushed individual efforts and hopes for a competent and independent living." "They lift up the rich and crush down the poor," it added, and thereby "will tolerate but two kinds of people—millionaires and paupers." Anticipating a Bryan victory in 1896, it urged children to "cheer up, for the day is already dawning when you can rightly hope to be something more than a corporation slave." Yet, elsewhere in the same issue, the *Argus* noted: Americans "do not wish to decrease the number of palaces; they are determined to increase the number of homes. They do not pray for harm to overtake the sons and daughters of plutocracy;

they are resolved that their own children shall have an opportunity to become worthy American citizens." Significantly, this charitable view stood virtually alone.[10]

The Wahoo paper stated, more typically: "In the second fifty years of the republic a new power grew up, unobserved by most men. . . Seated in the east, it has dominated the west and south, has monopolized legislation, fortified itself in the citadel of national power, and bids defiance to those who question its right." Thus, "the republic cannot live with an ever widening gulf between the rich and the poor." Even if "strife and bitterness" result, the path is clearly marked out: "The lover of his country will not yield sway to an arrogant, selfish, wealth-besotted oligarchy just because opposition or resistence may engender bitterness, strife or even war." Nor did this reveal a strain of conspiracy theory; two months later the same paper carefully distinguished between the "oligarchy" as individuals and as part of capitalism: "We are often asked why we are continually fighting the bankers, to which we reply that we are not fighting the bankers but the system and the political manipulators who have inaugurated and who are perpetuating the system." And as for the latter, "it is only a question of short time until the big fish will get them, too." The Broken Bow paper chose the invalidation of the income tax to sound its own warning: There is now "a system of debt slavery" in America; the Supreme Court "has declared for plutocratic wealth," with the result that "people have lost confidence in government and respect for law." The *Beacon* concluded, we "are approaching the temper of revolution." [11]

Momentarily leaving the midwest, one sees this same

view expressed by a Los Angeles attorney and retired colonel. Blanton Duncan, writing Ignatius Donnelly, observed: "Events are shaping themselves towards either a peaceable or the bloodiest sort of revolution. And it is for us to attempt to guide it *peacefully* if possible." Yet, Duncan goes on to reveal a curious ambivalence toward revolutionary activity. On one hand, it is unwise to encourage "in any manner the march of the poor" against those "who would be glad to shoot down the unemployed, under the pretense that it was anarchy and insurrection." The result would be frightening: "Any act of violence & murder would create such instant excitement & rising en masse of the starving multitude, that it might shake the Government to the foundations, and destroy half the values of the country, & send to death hundreds of thousands." Still, while such a move "was badly advised," it held out the only hope for showing "how utterly heartless, avaricious & damnable are the leaders & the 300 or 400000 of the rich & influential oligarchy who now own & control the Union." The next week he wrote Donnelly: "There is to be *civil war* in this country in my judgment *sure.*" [12]

Nor was this an isolated view; less than one month earlier the Topeka *Advocate* had cautioned: "Conditions are the same as preceded the French revolution, and unless a change is effected, and that very soon, the *result* will be the same." For the *Advocate* this was not an idle threat; the raw stuff of revolution—hunger and privation—was before its eyes: "Hungry men with starving wives and children have little conscience, and little regard for law, and it is useless to expect them to sit still and starve. They will never do it." And Eugene Debs,

sitting in his jail cell in the aftermath of Pullman, welcomed increased conflict as the means for stirring the
people. Going beyond Duncan, he wrote Lloyd: "The
one great result of this agitation has been to call the
attention of the country to the flagrant abuses of corporate power of which working people have so long
been the patient and uncomplaining victims." This was
no time to hesitate; man could finally affirm his dignity
through radical protest: "I am inclined to be optimistic
and do not hesitate to believe that all these things are
working together for the emancipation and redemption
of men from the thraldom that has so long held them in
slavery." This view was summed up by another of
Lloyd's correspondents: "I am full of courage and hope,
for the future rapid development of events, favorable to
an uprising for economic emancipation." [13]

And of course, the notion of ruling class was also
discussed frequently. "Organized interests," the *Alliance*
contended, not only controlled the major parties but
created artificial issues "to hide the hand that grasps
the wealth of the people with a grip of steel under a
velvet glove." In fact, capitalists stand above politics,
insuring that both parties are at one in reflecting their
demands: "Who does not know that no man can be
nominated for president by either party who is not
approved by the money power of New York and Boston, Who does not know that the railroad barons, democrats and republicans though they be, are ONE in the
halls of congress?" Thus, a consensus was enforced on
basic issues: "Who does not know that the protected
interests, belonging to all parties as they may, do not
jar against each other when a tariff bill is up?" Seven

months later this paper reprinted a Populist circular pointing out the tie between economic and political power: "Parallel with the tendency to concentrate wealth and commercial power in the hands of a small class has moved the tendency to concentrate political power in the same hands." Yet, this was not a plot; capitalism itself, through the pursuit of profit, developed a legal structure consistent with this goal. "To acquire money being the only inspiring motive, the effort is consistently being made to shape our laws to favor the classes who are combined on the money line." Populism, however, was seldom this dispassionate. Speaking of the Supreme Court in the next issue, the paper itself asserted: America "is building a Bastile to-day which is as purely the creation of the spirit of tyranny, which will be as surely the instrument of irresponsible power, and which will as surely crush out and blight the liberties of free-men as did that mute and horrid pile in Paris." In a more conspiratorial vein, the *Alliance* saw the power behind the throne as "immense, secret, cunning, unscrupulous," whose "representatives are the railroad kings and mil-lionaire bankers of the east." It is this group which is "packing the Supreme Court . . . to secure the undoing of all the great work" of the past. Here vagueness gives way to specific charges: "The granger decisions are reversed," and "the power of a state to regulate its own internal affairs has been denied." This is not an empty charge; self-evident cases, as when "Jay Gould demanded the appointment of Stanley Matthews to the Supreme bench," come to hand.[14]

Gould was indeed a favorite target; his well publicized gift to a New York church, the *Farmers' Alliance* suggested, was "less than his average daily robbery of the people." Worse, it was still accepted: "And a dozen divines and an equal number of his fellow robbers had a big banquet together over it at his house." The Wahoo paper was even more skeptical of philanthropy. Rockefeller's contribution to the University of Chicago, the *New Era* observed, was followed "almost immediately by a rise . . . in the price of oil," so that it "won't take him long to recoup that three millions." "When you grease your old wagon, or light your lamp tonight you ought to remember," it then quipped, "that you are contributing of your ten cent potatoes to the support of the Chicago University." Seven months later this paper maintained, in connection with Rockefeller's donation to Cleveland, Ohio: "What the people want is not gifts of charity, but simply an equal chance before the law and equal rights to nature's boundless gifts." Thus, ruling groups cannot hide behind philanthropy; there is "no need for that sort of charity where equal and exact justice for all rules." Or, as the Osceola paper simply asked, "Is it safe for a few individuals who have the wealth of this nation to control it?" A letter to Lewelling, though, best expressed the general feeling: The people must now decide whether they "will be governed by common consent, or yield obedience at the point of the bayonet to a soulless plutocracy." [15]

But the ruling class meant more than the sinister devil of Wall Street; for Populism this group was a statistical reality. S. S. King, in the pamphlet *Bond-Holders and Bread-Winners*, explained what Populism meant by the East and equivalent notions: "It is not against the East as a section nor against the masses of her people that the true reformer hurls his shafts." Rather, social protest is directed against the economic system itself, whose "fostered institutions of corruption" are "mainly located in the East." Using census data to measure the rate of economic growth during 1880–1890 for eastern and western states, King placed the concentration of wealth in the former area. Thus, "protest is necessarily entered against" this region "because our figures are of states and not individuals." The East becomes, then, the shorthand description of the power structure in the United States: Although "financial tyranny exists in the favored States, it is participated in by the few." The people, meanwhile, are left "to protest, or blinded and betrayed by sophistries, to submit." [16]

What, therefore, emerges from the comparison of Populism and Marxism? Since the similarities concern not superficial points but total views of capitalism, the following is clear: Populism, measured by Marx's own writings, offered a highly radical critique. Further, Populism can also be seen as more than an agrarian movement; its critique was possessed neither with the agrarian question nor the desire to turn back the clock on industrial development. But the comparison suggests even more; it provides fertile ground for historical imagination. Thus, the question immediately becomes, how can the similarities of totally independent systems of thought be explained—especially when lines of communication are absent, and intellectual roots so totally different? There are only two logical possibilities: chance, and the existence of similar historical contexts. Rejecting the first as unlikely, one confronts an extremely exciting prospect, perhaps even a new working hypothesis for determining the course of American history: If, in their respective periods, Populism and Marxism pointed to the same features of capitalism, it follows that capitalist development assumed the same pattern in the United States and Western Europe. In a word, the Populist experience might well challenge a basic proposition in historical writing—the uniqueness of America.

Henry D. Lloyd sensed this; capitalism is capitalism, on whichever side of the Atlantic. After complimenting Lloyd on his "deep sense of the importance of international movements," J. Keir Hardie observed: "Our troubles are the same all the world over." Sidney Webb reversed the order; America and Europe are comparable, but the former is actually more advanced: "In some respect the conflict between capital and labour takes in America an acuter form than with us, & with your rings and combines, you have reached a phase of economic development which we are only beginning." While Lloyd's correspondence is not typical of Populism, one sees here the breadth of contacts and maturity of discussion of the movement's leading intellectual.[17]

This is by way of introducing a final letter, in fact one of the most significant in American manuscript collections—Frederick Engels to Lloyd in 1893. Engels began, "Here in England modern Capitalism, during the century and a half of its full development, has lost much of its original brutal energy and moves onwards with a moderated step; even in France and Germany, this is to a certain degree the case also." Hence, earlier brutality gives way to more subtle forms of coercion; paradoxically, the revolutionary potential of radical groups decreases rather than increases with capitalist development:

"It is only in industrially young countries like America and Russia, that Capital gives full fling to the recklessness of its greed." Thus, change is possible only when oppression remains *known*; clearly Engels is stating a central point reached independently by many Populists. "The consolation, however, lies in this: That by this very recklessness it hurries on the developments of the immense resources of these young countries, and thereby prepares the period when a better system of production will be able to take the place of the old." For both Engels and Populism industrial America had reached the watershed; the fate of future society would be decided in the 1890's, or never again. Engels closed on a prophetic note—so wrong on its face, so right in the larger picture that protest would disappear when its moment was over: "In America, at least, I am strongly inclined to believe that the fatal hour of Capitalism will have struck as soon as a native American Working Class will have replaced a working class composed in its majority by foreign immigrants." Today there is a native working class, but no social protest. Were Populist fears therefore justified, that its defeat would mean the death knell of radicalism?[18]

CHAPTER FIVE

✤

SECTARIAN POLITICS

The Socialist Labor Party
Attack on Populism

One group in particular would deny the similarities of Populism and Marxism—American Marxists themselves. Yet, this counts for nothing; the Socialist Labor Party, the leading Marxist organization, was so blindly doctrinaire that Engels himself was prompted in 1894 to remark that it "managed to reduce the Marxian theory of development to a rigid orthodoxy, which the workers are not to reach themselves" but must "gulp down as an article of faith at once and without development." It is not surprising to find, then, that contemporary Marxists had one hard-and-fast position on Populism: It was the last gasp of the agrarian middle class.[1]

This very charge, however, inadvertently points up the reverse; its continual reiteration meant that the Socialist Labor Party saw in Populism a serious rival, and therefore a highly radical force. The party's executive committee report to the 1896 convention concedes as much: Populism "will be stripped of its socialistic pretentions" when it can "attain increased strength along the lines of its true character as a middle class movement." Here the "middle class" aspect can be seen as an act of faith, for the report continues: "It will cease to stand in our way and hinder the growth of our Party in Western states, where the allurements held out by Populist politicians served to give them quite a large following from among the working class." Thus, the elements of sectarian politics are ready at hand: The Socialist Labor Party admitted Populism expressed socialist principles and made inroads into the working class. And in explanation, it could only maintain that Populism was opportunistic, and the worker misguided.[2]

This position was elaborated in a campaign address, again a significant admission, to "the thinking and socialistic members and friends of the Populist party." Populism was the middle class protecting itself both from the rising industrialists and the workers: "We are cognizant of the fact that the Populist movement is the result of certain economic conditions—of a historical struggle for existence between the middle class and the modern capitalist class of exploiters of Labor and profit-hunters." Yet, these selfsame economic tendencies will also destroy Populism, once it has outlived its usefulness. "But we also recognize the fact that the same economic and natural laws that produced the Populist movement of the present day will, in a short course of time, bring about the unavoidable downbreak and dissolution of the People's Party." Therefore, "the efforts of the People's Party to save the middle class from ruin and destruction will be futile." Interestingly enough, the address then contradicted itself; Populism did contain non-middle class elements: "The conflicting material class interests represented by the different factions in the People's Party will cause the final destruction of that party, since it will be impossible to harmonize said diametrically opposed class interests." Two points emerge here. Recognizing the complexity of Populism, the Socialist Labor Party nonetheless continued to label the movement as middle class; further, its contention that radicals and conservatives existed side-by-side is a truism applicable to many large-scale social movements. It failed to discuss, however, the proportions of each in Populism.[3]

Paul Ehrmann, a Chicago socialist, was more incisive, arguing not from an a priori rejection of Populism but an appraisal of its actual program. He challenged Lloyd on whether the Populist endorsement of "nationalization of R Roads, Telephone, Telegraphs, Savings banks and Public improvements" means "the Working Class will cease to be exploited." "Your own logic and knowledge of Political economy," Ehrmann added, "will convince you that this form of governmental proprietorship does not abolish the Wages system." Yet, here one sees the orthodoxy Engels warned against; because Populism does not stand for total collectivization it must be wholly reactionary: "Those measures are merely aids for the continuance of the competitive struggle of the middle class against their powerful antagonist class the Capitalist." The Socialist Labor Party never queried whether the specific socialist measures Populism *did* adopt would fundamentally alter industrial capitalism. Instead, as Ehrmann suggests, these were capitalist proposals in disguise: "Governmental ownership of the public utilities you mention will cheapen the cost of transporting the products of the individualistic farmer to a market which affords him an enhanced profit." Further, "Governmental Banks of deposit, Telephones and Telegraphs are all aids to support the competitive struggle of the hard-pressed middle class." Hence, Populists will "accept seemingly radical planks," but "only those that will enable them to continue on in an improved condition to carry on this system of exploitation." [4]

But Daniel De Leon, ideologue-leader of the party, expressed by far the most interesting view. Taking Lewelling's "Tramp Circular" as his point of departure, De Leon stressed the radical aspects of Populism. This did not, however, yield an ambivalent conclusion, still less a willingness to work with the movement. Instead, in true sectarian fashion, Populism was damned as reactionary. Hence, writing two and a half years before the 1896 convention, De Leon recognized the radical potential in Populism—and promptly turned his back. "The Populist movement," he began, "was born in the West, and only there did it have whatever vitality it once possessed." Thus, it was agrarian and middle class, and nothing more: "It was a middle class movement, a movement aiming at the impossible achievement of preserving the system of small production." Populism had nothing whatever for the worker: "Accordingly, while it uttered grandiloquent and unmeaning phrases on behalf of the wage workers, it talked very concrete language on behalf of the small producers, farmers especially, whose limited acreage and capital rendered them unequal to the competitive struggle."

Then came the about-face; while conservative Populists advocated "cheap money," others in the movement supported "more genuinely radical demands, looking to

the public ownership of the instruments of production"
and minimizing "financial ones." In fact, "This split is
becoming more and more apparent." On one hand, "the
money fanatics attribute more and more firmly all our
industrial misfortunes to the absence of a sufficient per
capita of money." But on the other, "the more enlightened, or radical element . . . is talking less and less about
a per capita of money as THE CAUSE of prosperity or
misery," and is turning instead "to the real question—
the private or monopolistic ownership of machinery and
all other necessities of production." De Leon conceded
even more; Lewelling's statement gives proof of "this
evolution in the ranks of Populism." There is "not a word
here about a reduced per capita throwing men out of
work!" He then quoted, and emphasized, these words in
the proclamation: "The *monopoly of labor-saving machinery* and its devotion to selfish instead of *social* use,
have rendered more and more human beings superfluous." As for this wing of Populism, then, "the cause of
pauperism is soundly set forth." De Leon concluded,
"Gov. Lewelling belongs to that wing of Populism that
is moving onwards and that is bound one day to stand
shoulder to shoulder with the . . . Socialists." Yet, De
Leon never eased up in his attack; the party organ, *The
People*, often appeared more anti-Populist than anti-
capitalist.[5]

The party position is clear; additional evidence only
refines the basic pattern. That De Leon, an extremely
hostile source, saw radical dimensions to Populism underscores the sectarian response of the Socialist Labor Party.
Rather than attack major parties, it engaged, as one
member reported, in activities such as the "Debate on

Populism vs. Socialism," in which "Daniel the Lion" showed "that populism would not only [not] benefit but positively injure the working men." And there was ample reason for bitterness; each movement competed for the same support. A district secretary-treasurer of the United Mine Workers in Illinois makes this clear. He wrote a Socialist Labor Party organizer: "I am a socialist myself, but as there has never been a ticket in the field here to vote for I have voted the Peoples Party ticket, as the nearest approach to socialism." Thus, "The socialistic sentiments in its platform is all that holds me in it." This points up not only radical, but specifically labor-radical, support for Populism.[6]

J. Wilson Becker, the organizer in question, was himself in the midwest trying to wean away radical Populists —without success. In mid-June of 1896 Becker notified the party secretary: "I have met here [Ohio] a wonderful mixture of Ideas The Pops roundly denounced me because I said in reply to this question—Would you support E. V. Debs for President on the Populist Platform. I replied no." He then complained, "I can't get these Damn fools to accept the class struggle, all they call for is *fusion, fusion,* fusion they wont see anything until it hits them." But even Becker had misgivings over party policy: "Prospects poor to organize all yelling for their Tin God Debs, and wearing his buttons. It seems that this is the only hope of the Radicals is to try and stampede the men toward Debs." As Becker's report ten days later suggests, socialists within Populism had no misgivings until the very end—July 1896—when William Jennings Bryan was endorsed. "I find that lots of so-called Pop-Socialists are hanging off awaiting the result of the

St. Louis Populist convention renders my work hard."
Hence, for six years avowed socialists regarded Populism
as a suitable expression of their goals; only with fusion
did this change.[7]

A radical Populist from Texas best summed up the
feeling of the group. Writing to Charles Matchett, Socialist Labor Party candidate for president, he stated,
"I am and have been a Straight Middle of the road
Populist, but since the St. Louis convention am at Sea
and without a rudder or compass I would like to have
a copy of your National Platform . . . with a view of
voting your ticket in November." Still, even he would
remain in the Populist movement, if a substitution were
offered for Bryan. "In case there is no Straight out
Populist in the field my vote will likely go to your Party
there are others holding my views that could probably
be induced to vot your ticket." Another non-midwest-
erner described the situation this way: "In common with
a vast number of people I thought that the Peoples Party
was traveling toward the Cooperative Commonwealth.
Events sometimes open ones eyes wide and quick. The
St. Louis convention to which I was a delegate performed
that office for me." He then observed, "I learned that
all the leaders desired nothing more than to 'reform'
(patch up) the present system." Parenthetically, this
view was itself incorrect; as the last chapter of this book
will show, Populists conceived fusion in highly radical
terms. Be that as it may, defections occurred *with* fusion,
and not before. In fact, the Socialist Labor Party prior
to this time was fighting for its very survival. One
socialist informed De Leon: "It is an all around acknowl-
edged fact that the Socialists of the city [San Francisco]

were the main reason for the populist movement in this place; it was therefore not a small struggle for the S.L.P. to stand on her own feet in our last municipal election." [8]

Finally, competition sometimes led to vengeance; a Minneapolis socialist promised De Leon that labor would support the party—or no one. "Our work," he began, "is mainly in the direction of disciplinizing first our own members," since many of them have "been demoralized by the previous connections with the P.P." Hence, "We have adopted the resolution as to entering into political action, and excluding members for doing anything for the Pops." Here one sees Populism always in the foreground—as chief rival, as recruiting ground, as magnet attracting restive socialists. Accordingly, "And if we fail to have the Trades and Labor Council endorse our ticket when proper time for it comes, we will surely prevent it from indorsing the People's Party." Better to drag down the entire American left, this member suggested by his action, than allow the Populist movement a foothold in labor.[9]

But a still better reason exists than sectarian conduct to discount the Socialist Labor Party critique: The *positive* side of Populism itself reveals the existence of socialist threads. Starting from the "gas and water" variety, the Topeka *Advocate* explained the character of Populist socialism. "The best features of our government today," it began, "national, state and municipal, are those which are purely socialistic." This was hardly radical, though, for the paper cited "our public school system and our postal system" as the "exemplification of pure socialism." At first sight, then, purity meant a highly innocuous form, chiefly confined to public utilities: "Municipal ownership of waterworks, gas works, electric light plants, and other public utilities by which the people receive the maximum of service for a minimum of cost afford other examples of pure socialism, by which serious abuses are corrected and great benefits secured to the public." Yet, this kind of socialism was only the groundwork, and by no means an end in itself. "It is undoubtedly true that observing and studious Populists with such examples before them, have come to believe that a still wider extension of socialistic doctrines and practices would be beneficial to mankind." Thus, Populism had no fixed position. This was a pragmatic creed, groping for basic solutions: "Looking about them they see nearly every industry monopolized by a corporation," so that "they are conscious of the robbery practiced upon them for private gain." The answer was paternalism, a non-doctrinaire socialism developing in response to existing conditions: "They have come to believe that many of the abuses to which they are subject might be remedied, and their condition bettered by a proper exercise of the power of the government." [10]

Less than three months later this paper flatly stated, "Public ownership of railroads, telegraphs, telephones, and all other utilities now monopolized or susceptible of being monopolized . . . would inure to the benefit of the people." Here, then, was a further refinement; the very existence of monopoly warrants a close, hard look: It was "therefore the *duty* of the government . . . to *assume* the ownership and management of all such utilities and monopolies in the interest of the public." And nine months later, referring to this "false and malicious industrial system," the *Advocate* laid down the following rule:

The solution was "public control of these means of production and a sufficient reduction of the hours of labor
to afford every willing hand an opportunity to work,
thereby giving the benefits of improved methods to labor
rather than permit capital to absorb vast profits and turn
labor out to starve." [11]

Still, this was now the close of 1894, when Populist
views had begun to crystallize. The earlier statements
are even more interesting, for they indicate the roots of
this later conception. The Broken Bow, Nebraska, paper
observed in 1889, "As to socialism, in its ideal condition,
it would be a realization of the millennium." Hence, one
finds distrust as to the practicality of socialism, but not
hostility for its principles: "We are not opposed to socialism—yet as a practical solution of present day problems
. . . we are somewhat inclined to pronounce socialism
too far in the future." In a breeding ground such as this,
where opposition is based on tactics and not goals, the
possibilities for more radical action are clearly manifest:
"We must deal with actual people and practical questions until the ideal people are created and the theories
of socialism become practical." Time, experience, and
worsening conditions were still needed; the stage, however, had been set. [12]

A letter to the *Farmers' Alliance* in 1890 denied the
remoteness of socialism—for factory *and* farm: There
are "two classes of men who are ripe for socialism," the
urban poor and "the farmer renters." Their interests are
identical, for both "are fast approaching the same condition." Thus, socialism becomes a reality because "the
line between land lord and tenant is being forcibly put
as the line of demarkation is now drawn in the cities

between boss and employe." Three years later the
Alliance-Independent, demonstrating its awareness of
European socialism, praised German "social democracy"
in these terms: It has "organized for the complete over-
throw of the capitalistic system." Further, it did "not
commit the monumental folly of 'keeping out of politics.' " Of the two, however, only the latter was relevant
for Populism; praise was one matter, revolution quite
another. "Here," it warned, "is a lesson the masses of
America must learn." They cannot "remain ignorant or
poorly informed as to the great fundamental truths of
political economy and government," and they cannot
"eschew independent political action." So long as these
conditions persist, so long "will the American masses
be the prey of the money power." While the "truths"
involved here meant socialism, their pursuit was clearly
a laborious process: "When the farmers and laboring
men of America learn by long and patient study just
what they want, when they organize to get it no matter
how long it may take, when they learn to stand by their
leaders and their organs . . . they will succeed, but not
till then." For Populism, therefore, socialism was a long,
difficult and unclear road, but one not to be rejected out
of hand.[13]

Perhaps Henry D. Lloyd best expressed the relation
of Populism and socialism. "I have never identified myself," he wrote the president of Iowa College, "with the
Socialists as an organization." But "if I were in England
I should certainly have affiliated with the Fabian society."
For Lloyd the Socialist Labor Party repelled the American radical; his decision was dictated by a revulsion for
"the hard tone of the German Socialists, who are about

all we have." He objected most to "the doctrine they constantly reiterate that this crisis must be met by a class struggle," in which "the working people alone are to be trusted." Thus, "instead of joining the Socialists as an organization, I have joined the People's Party." [14]

Nor is Lloyd's own radicalism to be doubted; as early as 1890 he used socialism as the standard for rejecting current reform sentiments as superficial. Henry George, Lloyd related to a friend, saw "neither the cause nor the cure of our social problem." In fact, "the effect of putting all the taxes on land would be infallibly to shift its possession to those who had the money to pay the taxes." Free trade was no more desirable: "The Free Trade commonly clamored for is simply a widening of the field for competition, and is the last act in a drama of trade run mad." This was the attempt of a "commerce crazy" society desperately seeking to iron out its business cycles, a society thinking "that the collapses caused by drunken indulgence in buying cheap (so called) and selling dear (so called) would be cured by a larger dose of the same stimulant." Free trade was therefore imperialism. Not unlike Marx, Lloyd suggested that expanded operations —"a widening of the field for competition"—was the means through which capitalism resolves, or postpones, internal difficulties. Nor does the similarity end here; Lloyd criticized the term "free" in free trade in a manner reminiscent of Marx's attack on "freedom" under commodity production: "Free trade that is free, will be a trade where the barter is of articles that were freely made as well as freely traded, and 'freely' means in obedience to true laws of honor, health, and beauty." Lloyd bluntly added, "Trade that exchanges the products of slave labor, whether of plantation or slum, cannot be free." Hence, "Our bourgeoissie do not care how or where things are made, so long as by swapping them" one can "be 'free' to become rich at the cost of poverty to others."

Then, rejecting protectionism as "provincial, worse, parochial," Lloyd observed: "The workingmen and their friends care nothing for this question of tariff so dear to the business man." Instead, and here his own radical stand becomes apparent, "when they [workers] reign," they will replace protection with "a system of industry, internationally cooperative, a real free trade, because bottomed on a brotherhood, which recognizes that the common toil of mankind, must, and can be, so directed as to give the necessities of life to all before it gives yachts and champagne to any." Lloyd closed with a truly dialectical flourish; free trade must be encouraged so that the economic system will crumble all the more rapidly: "I should hasten Free Trade in our present system because it would internationalize more completely" the economic system, and thus "would make the breakdown, so accelerated, take place on the same field where the reconstruction must go on—the field of the internation." [15]

Thus, very often only a fine line separated Populism from socialism. Lloyd, after all, *was* a Populist; this can be seen by his own admission, and the fact that he ran for Congress on the People's party ticket in 1894. In fact, his campaign superbly illustrated the urban dimensions of Populism, for here practically all shades of radicalism could and did merge. Willis J. Abbot, a prominent journalist still holding radical views at this time, wrote

Lloyd: "I feel that Chicago this winter is going to be a fruitful field for socialistic agitation." Lloyd never hoped to win, but the educational opportunities of the campaign could not be bypassed. And Debs warmly endorsed him in these terms: "Only wish there were a Lloyd in every Congressional District in the country." [16]

The campaign aftermath, however, revealed even more clearly Lloyd's position on socialism. At this time he clarified his views in an exchange of letters with Clarence Darrow. Dejected by the conviction of American Railway Union members, and disillusioned by the campaign, Darrow confided that he was "in a quandry about the Peoples Party." He explained, "I might be willing to join a Socialist party but I am not willing to help in another Socialist movement under the guise of the Peoples Party' we must take some stand or drop out altogether." Lloyd countered, "The course of the socialists in Chicago deserves sympathetic attention." Still cool to the De Leon faction, he added: "Contrary to all their past politics, their predilections, and the threats and persuasions of the party's leaders elsewhere, as in New York," they gave "up their political identity, and went in with all their might for the success of the People's Party." Then came the central point: "The People's Party platform is socialistic, as all democratic doctrine is." Darrow was unduly pessimistic; Populists and socialists can establish a working basis, a firm coalition. "No question of principle is involved in the admission of the Socialists as full and regular members of the People's Party. They are the most intelligent, most energetic, most reliable workers we have." This was not the time to disavow socialist support; to do so "would be to repeat the blunder Henry George made at the State convention in Syracuse some years ago." "They were willing to cooperate with him," Lloyd continued, "but to save himself the odium of 'socialistic' affiliations he excluded them from the convention—and he has never been heard of since as a political force." Lloyd closed on a bold note; Populism must seize control of the American left and make radicalism a vital force: "Our cue is to get the Socialists of other states to do as the Chicago socialists have done. That makes Chicago the intellectual and political leader of this movement." [17]

Finally, the fate of Populists dissatisfied with Bryan's nomination in 1896 further bears out the socialist potential within Populism. Left without a movement, many in this "middle-of-the-road" (non-fusion) group gravitated to the Socialist Labor Party. Hence, until 1896, there *were* Populists holding socialist views while remaining consistent Populists. The chairman of a Kansas People's party county committee wrote the national secretary of the Socialist Labor Party: "The Demo Plutocracy have closed the mouths of our leaders by nomination for office." Because the leadership has been bought off, he continued, "the rank and file of the middle of the Road Populists (in reality Socialists) are raging and I am sure a S.L.P. ticket would poll 10,000 votes in Kansas this year." It was no longer possible to hold radical views; the endorsement of Bryan "was the straw that broke the campbells back." The writer then anticipated the deeply-grained bias of many socialists. "Do not think," he asserted, "that because our people are agriculturists that therefore they are not socialists. I myself was born and raised a farmer but I can count 50 socialists amoung my old farm neighbors." [18]

Likewise, the secretary of a local People's party committee in Colorado wrote the same socialist leader: "Our party (Populist) in Colorado is pretty badly disorganized —or perhaps *dissatisfied* would better express it." Thus, "While I look for the bulk of the party vote to go to the Electoral ticket to be named next week it will be done under protest, and after the November election voters will begin to rearrange themselves, and on Socialist lines." Two weeks later he incisively added: "The voters here realize that Populism, the majority party here, is irrevocably divided, and that the logical end of the radical element is in socialism." Still, radical Populists could not now leave the party: "But they also realize that so far as this *present* campaign is concerned, the fight is between Bryan and McKinely." There was no other choice. "Knowing as they do," he concluded, "that each represents only a part, both of which are evil, still they prefer the lesser evil of the two and will vote for Bryan —in fact to do otherwise would seem a species of treason." Or as a letter from Lynden, Washington, simply expressed the situation: "This was a Strong Pop County a great many of us wanted to be sure why we wer pops and it mad Socialists of us there are a great many, undeveloped Socialists shoing up since the Convensions." [19]

One question remains: Was fusion, the endorsement of Bryan in 1896, a conservative departure or a betrayal of principle? Was Populism therefore a middle class movement all along, or at best radical only in its early stages? Fusion, then, is the crucial test of Populist radicalism. If the policy was conservative, Populism cannot in the long run be taken as a truly radical force. Clearly, conservative ripples can be detected by spring 1895; at this time Illinois Populism purged its socialist wing. The plight of Thomas J. Morgan, a leading Chicago socialist, demonstrated this. When Lloyd sought his services for the 1896 campaign, Morgan bitterly replied: "In regard to the P.P. Even if their convention results as you wish (which I doubt), It is no place for me." Morgan added, "I am a socialist, cannot be known or understood as anything else, and as such even the Radical P.P.s think my work in their behalf should be unseen and unheard even they would mutinee against 'Morgan the Orator.' " Yet, by itself, this does not suggest that Populism had become transformed.[20]

The discussion of fusion must begin with the political realities of 1896: Did support of Bryan signify a conservative or an opportunistic course, when to remain independent would insure McKinley's election? Here a letter—not from a Populist moving toward socialism but the reverse, a member of the Socialist Labor Party breaking away to join Populism—places the problem in focus. Explaining to his state central committee that "for six years I have faithfully discharged my duties as a member," the writer based his decision to leave on the ground "that the time has fully come to take an advanced step along political lines." Thus, "If ever the Co-operative Commonwealth is to be achieved the true reformer must take advantage of every opportunity presented. As the S.L.P. of America can never grow beyond the limit of certain nationalities the cause of socialism will never progress in its present condition." And if the party cannot bring socialism to America, socialists must work through other parties—and precisely now. "The time has come," he asserted, "to recognize this need and meet the demand." In fact, "that party has come to us; if it wins, Socialism is all the quicker to be achieved, if it loses the cause of the wage slave is retarded at least twenty-five years." This new political force was Democratic-Populist fusion, expressed by the Democratic platform: "I see a brighter hope of victory for the enslaved masses in the Chicago platform and its candidate." Only sectarianism blinds the socialist to the radical possibilities in the new situation. "A party to be successful, must . . . be committed to a principal, but it must also have men of principal at its head and to its support; men who can see beyond their own personal interests, beyond their own little fields of action." Thus, this long-time socialist summed up, the charge of Populism as a middle class movement was a red herring: "The so called middle class of people are the ones who are taking up your issues and carrying them to success. You may slander and misrepresent them, as some of your leaders do, but the facts remain the same." Was fusion therefore a sell-out? [21]

✣

CHAPTER SIX

FUSION

The Last Assertion
of Populist Radicalism

Fusion was a desperate move. Populism had passed its peak; to avoid the fate of other third parties, it now had only one course open—to strive for major party status. Otherwise, all it stood for would wither away. Fusion meant not the spoils of office but the last chance to advance radicalism. It meant not capitulation but the resounding affirmation of principle. Populism was not deluded; it recognized that long years of agitation could be erased in a stroke. Radical to the bitter end, it took the risk with wide-open eyes—and failed miserably. The result was a paradox and a tragedy; everything Populism sought to avoid came about. Repudiating free silver for more radical demands, it was forced to support a silver crusade. Trying to remain independent and avoid extinction, it became absorbed by the Democratic party and was destroyed. Having grave reservations on Bryan, it formed the backbone of his following. No, third parties do not fare well in the American political system—nor at the hands of historians. Fusion was both a necessity and an agent of destruction; and when the smoke has cleared, and no party remains, historians see this as proof of conservatism. Yet, Populism declined because it was too radical, and not too conservative. The two-party structure insured its demise.

Henry D. Lloyd, himself the arch-critic of fusion in the closing weeks of the campaign, described the People's party convention in precisely this way. Fusion was the attempt to consolidate radicalism "until ready for a more decisive advance." It was a highly positive step to place goals above party, for Populism "is composed altogether of men who had already had the self-discipline of giving up party for the sake of principle." The purpose was not to water down radicalism; Bryan's nomination was founded on the "solicitude to do nothing which should hinder the Rising of the People, if that had really begun." Nor did free silver define the core of fusion sentiment. While Lloyd later denounced the measure for crowding out radical demands, he was well aware that this was not anticipated during the convention. Hence, Populism did not seek fusion to achieve free silver. Even though the People's party and silver conventions met the same time in the same city, "the silver convention exercised no influence on that of the Populists." In fact, the latter "convention cared less for silver than did the Democratic convention." Although "most of the Democrats really believe free silver is a great reform," Populists think very differently. Populists admit in private that "silver was only the most trifling installment of reform, and many—a great many—did not conceal their belief that it was no reform at all."

Lloyd then pointed out an interesting fact: This very convention responsible for fusion contained a substantial proportion of the more radical Populists. "If the issue had been made," he continued, "there was an even chance" of selecting a ticket based upon "a platform far in advance of that adopted in Omaha in 1892, one demanding, for instance, the public ownership of all monopolies." Why therefore did Populism swallow Bryan, fusion, and free silver when there was sufficient support for remaining independent? Very simply, Populism had its back to the wall; there was no other way to preserve radicalism. The radical leaders at the convention were "formidable enough to have split the convention near the middle, if not to have carried it." Yet, they did not lift a finger. These men (he singled out Coxey, Waite, and Peffer) "did not lead, and their followers did not clamor to be led." Recalling Lloyd's own undoubted radicalism, one must carefully weigh his explanation for fusion: "The fear ruled that unless the reform forces united this time they would never again have the opportunity to unite. It was in the air that there must be union. The footfall of the hour for action was heard approaching." Radicalism must strike now, or perhaps never again. "It was a psychological moment of *rapprochement* against an appalling danger which for thirty years now had been seen rising in the sky." Lloyd closed, "If the radicals made a mistake, it was a patriotic mistake." [1]

There was no pattern to fusion; Populists differed on timing, reasons for its adoption, and intensity of commitment. This diversity hardly suggests that fusion was a sudden about-face or the result of a rigged convention. Instead, it was a long-term groping toward effective radical action.

The Topeka *Advocate*, in the radical vanguard of

Populism, is an excellent case study. "While the demand for free coinage of silver," the paper observed in November 1893, "is one of the planks of the Omaha platform, it is the one of least importance among them all." Silver alone is a mockery, for "it is only in conjunction with other measures that it would afford relief." First, the dominant groups must be removed; otherwise, free silver will merely intensify the concentration of wealth: "The men who now corner gold, would, under their administration, also corner silver." Hence, as the *Advocate* noted one month later, silver can be effective only when part of a larger program: "We want, not simply more money, but what is of far greater importance, in itself considered, we want an entire revolution in our system, and in the conduct of public affairs." Any effort to subordinate Populism to silver "is inspired by the all potent spirit of plutocracy." Two weeks later, the start of 1894, the paper again attacked free silver: "We want no sham battles or victories that will be barren of results." Thus, Populists at an early date exposed silver as superficial; yet, paradoxically, historians often attack these same Populists for not recognizing the superficiality of silver. The *Advocate* continued: "There must be a complete revolution of our social system to make it conform to the new conditions resulting from the adoption of labor-saving machinery and modern methods of production and distribution." Here silver was worse than ineffective; it obscured more basic issues. "It is folly . . . to think that a simple change in our money system will remedy the evils from which we are suffering." The change, in fact, "would only add to the accumulations of capitalists and to their power to further oppress the people." [2]

In March 1895 the *Advocate* was still hostile to silver. It reminded the recently organized silver party, "The issues are clearly drawn" not only between the major parties and Populism, "but they are no less clearly drawn between the new party and our own." What use had Populism for the single plank? Populism was growing, and the increase had nothing to do with "the question of free silver or any other phase of the financial question." Instead, it reflected "the widespread sentiment in favor of public ownership of public utilities." Further, "it was a revolt against the abuses of monopoly, and the arbitrary exercise of the powers of government through the courts and the army in trampling under foot the rights and the liberties of the people." Radicalism, not silver, was responsible for this growth. And if anything, Populism was becoming more, not less, radical: "Circumstances have changed somewhat since 1892, and we believe the people will favor a *broadening* rather than a narrowing of the platform." Thus, "We will need to be more explicit in our declarations against the monopoly of land and, in short, the three great fundamental questions of finance, land and transportation in all their essential phases must continue to distinguish the People's party from all other political organizations." The *Advocate* concluded, "Every monopoly must be operated by the public and for the public good." [3]

Skipping ahead to June 1896, some six weeks before the People's party convention, one finds the paper still opposed to fusion with silver as its basis: "There are other things to be condemned besides the demonetization of silver." Rather, the main issues were corporate domination, technological unemployment ("not more than

25 per cent. of the mechanics and tradesmen of the country are working full time at full wages"), and high interest rates. "The free coinage of all the silver that all the mines of the world produce," it continued, would not be enough "if unaccompanied by other reforms." Hence, "Populists will not unite with any party or with any factions that go no farther than silver." Or as it observed the next week: "If there were nothing at stake but the silver question, the Populist party would not have come into existence." [4]

Four weeks later the *Advocate* endorsed fusion. Nor was this a conservative or an opportunistic shift. It began, "Events of the last four weeks have so changed the political situation that a grave responsibility has been suddenly thrust upon the Populist party." Until now no one could anticipate the Republican party's threat to American society: "The Republican National convention boldly and plainly espoused the cause of the money power—the most dangerous agency of oppression which ever cursed mankind." This "means war on the industries of the people; it means class rule, oppression of the poor— debt, poverty, perpetual enslavement of the masses." At the same time, again unforeseen, "a majority of the Democrat party have lifted themselves out of the old ruts and have grandly risen to a higher level." Thus, there can be no hesitation: "Populists are confronted with a grave responsibility" to stop McKinley. "They have," it went on, "votes enough when united with those of other friends of silver, to win this battle for the people." This came one week *before*, not during or after, the People's party convention, suggesting that radicals were not simply stampeded on the convention floor.

Fusion, whatever the machinations of conservative leaders, had deeper roots. With the campaign the *Advocate*
grew more enthusiastic. "Let us combine temporarily,"
it urged one week after the convention, "with men who
think as we do about the issue which has been forced
upon the country by the alliance of the Republican party
with the gold syndicate." And the next week it added,
"The first thing the convention did was to adopt its own
party platform; and that document shows our principles
as distinguished from those of other parties." Further,
the vice presidential candidate is "a Populist of the
straightest sect," and the presidential candidate, "a man
who is a Populist in everything else but the name." The
paper therefore did not regard fusion as a sell-out.[5]

This was not campaign rhetoric. The *Advocate* explained more fully just before the election: "Last June
the country was brought face to face with a proposition
to perpetuate our present ruinous financial policy, and
that is the only issue in this campaign." Populism did not
seek out fusion and free silver; the Republican platform
"renders it necessary on the part of the opposition to a
permanent gold standard to make common cause" against
this threat. Significantly, at this late date, the paper still
insisted there was a basic difference between Populists
and Democrats: "We do not believe in the use of money
that has to be redeemed in coin." Populism stood not for
free silver but for "all of the money of the country to be
good and of equal purchasing and debt-paying power."
Hence, Populism was committed to free silver for one
reason only: "No other or further step can be taken
toward monetary reform until the silver question is
properly disposed of." The paper then summed up where

Populism fitted into the fusion argument: "This is as far as the Democrats now propose to go, and it is as far as the Populists could go, because Republicans have tendered that as the pending issue." [6]

The *Advocate*, like most of Populism, was well intentioned in supporting fusion; it never once sacrificed its radical principles. When the end came, it was wholly innocent of what had happened. "That Populism was the force," the paper commented after the election, "which brought new life to Democracy and brought about a separation of the discordant elements in that organization, there is no room for doubt." On this it was correct. But it never sensed that Populism was now dead. Instead, it justified fusion to the bitter end: "The times were ripe for a coming together of like elements in all the great parties, because an issue had risen on which men in the several parties had well defined but opposite views, and the issue was deemed by all to be vital." Fusion was never intended to sabotage Populist radicalism. The *Advocate* concluded on a note clearly demonstrating that the movement declined through no conscious effort of Populists themselves. This, they naively believed, was only the start of a more all-embracing radicalism: "The time is now at hand when Populists may hopefully move for an effective union of all elements that are opposed to a system of finance which operates to put and keep the governing forces of the country in the hands of comparatively a few persons." [7]

The Lincoln *Farmers' Alliance*, under its later names, adopted a similar stand on fusion. "*What we have come together on*," it noted as the *Alliance-Independent* in early 1894, "must be held intact." Fusion must be resisted at all costs: "Politics and politicians are not wanted. Cutting and trimming, compromising and fusing, are suicidal." One year later, as the *Wealth Makers*, the paper restated its opposition: "Fusion, contracting with those who are not Populists, is betrayal of the people's trust, is 'the densest political stupidity,' if party principle is of any value." The next week saw a scathing attack on silver: "Free silver would not lower rents, would not reduce transportation tribute, would not curb the power of the Standard Oil trust, would not destroy the monopoly in coal or lumber, or steel, or sugar, or dressed meats . . . would not reduce the usuary tribute, or money and wealth concentration." Basic Populist principles, not the shallow single plank, were needed: "Cut off the power of monopolies by means of government banks, railroads, coal mines, telegraphs, etc., and something great and permanent is accomplished." For those seeking a compromise, the *Wealth Makers* advised, "Get out of the Populist party, or quit trying to pull its platform to pieces. . . The 2,000,000 men who have come together on the Omaha platform will stand no scheming to get them off it." Or as a letter to the editor maintained in that same issue, "We say to the little great men who would sidetrack the Populist party on non-essentials: hands off the Omaha platform." The People's party, it continued, "will become a radical, aggressive party, boldly attacking the strongholds of the money power, under the lead of great men who appreciate its mission." [8]

In February 1895 the *Wealth Makers* itself equated fusion with conservatives. The "one-idea men" were urging "that it is policy for us to slip out of sight those stumbling stones and rocks of offense in our platform that are called socialistic, viz., the demand for the government ownership of the railroads, telegraphs, telephones and banks." But the group was small and had little support. "The Populist party press, state and national organs, we happen to know, is almost to the last paper unchanged in its devotion to the Populist principles embraced in the Omaha platform." Hence, as of early 1895 anti-fusion sentiment still prevailed. The paper noted in April, "Now is the time for the Populists to show emphatically that free silver is not all they demand, nor the greater part, and that we know better than to reduce our platform to one idea, an idea which would enable the Democratic party to smear and swallow us." The choice was clear: "Silver with us is an incidental. Government ownership of the great monopolies is our main idea." [9]

The next week a letter from Red Cloud, Nebraska, suggested free silver was worthless, so "long as the trusts and monopolies are on top and the banks have the same facilities to concentrate the money." Instead, "We will get permanent relief only when the government owns the railroads and when we have government banks where we can get money at a small rate of interest. Under these circumstances it would be worse than foolish for us to give up the Omaha platform." A second letter to the editor was more direct: "If our platform tinkerers would take a few grains of podophylline for the 'swell-head' they would experience a feeling of relief, to which they have long been strangers." Referring also to the Omaha platform, it concluded: "Every plank of that inspired document is needed for the relief of the people; anything less would fail to hold the vast army of voters that wish to stand upon it." [10]

The paper, now the *Nebraska Independent*, still opposed fusion in April 1896; three months remained before the People's party convention. "These democratic free silver men," it warned, "will be woefully disappointed if they base their hopes on the idea that any considerable number of populists can, by any means, be induced to vote for a democratic candidate for president." Then, in July, the change came; Bryan's nomination on a radical Democratic platform was decisive. In the interim between the Democratic and People's conventions the paper polled its readers on what course to follow. Here the change in attitude is precisely pinpointed. One, angry because the Democratic nominee is "nearer a populist than any other man in their party, and their platform is stolen from ours," conceded: "We cannot afford to defeat him. Two years more of Sherman and Clevelandism means too much suffering." The respondent concluded, "Populists must sacrifice their pride for the good of their country." Another letter was more positive: "The opportunity is now offered to elect a president standing on the platform containing all the populist principles at issue in this campaign. What more could we ask?" A third reply called for fusion for an entirely different reason; it would serve as an object-lesson against any future attempts of this kind: "The free coinage of silver would only give temporary relief at most. Let them get sick even unto death. Experience is the best and safest teacher." The prevalent view, however, was that fusion alone could make possible the defeat of McKinley. One letter flatly stated, "The St. Louis convention must choose between McKinley and Bryan." Another letter held, "In my opinion a division in the reform forces at this time would only contribute towards the election of McKinley." A final letter summed up the referendum: "No personal or party selfishness should influence patriotic citizens to divide forces and permit wrong to triumph." These are the voices of rank-and-file Populists, and *before* the People's party convention.[11]

The *Independent* agreed. One week after the convention it maintained, "The peoples party . . . has not been swallowed by the democracy and the democracy has not been swallowed by it. The two organizations stand as distinct from each other as they ever did." Fusion was only a short-term course: "What has been done is an agreement during this campaign that we will unite our forces for a supreme effort to elect W. J. Bryan president of these United States." And only through a Bryan victory were more basic reforms possible, for "he will throw the almost omnipotent power of this great government against the national banks, against the oppression of the corporations and against the money power." The paper further explained in August, "All Populists agree that legislation cannot be given a trend in this direction [of the Omaha platform] until the government is wrested from the control of the money power." This, then, was the order of priority—first, fusion and silver as a stepping stone, and "after that, we march on." Fusion must be supported, it went on the next week, because "the only hope of the common people is the success of Bryan. With Bryan defeated and McKinley elected no man can imagine the misery that will follow." The election only one month away, the *Independent* continued to urge Populists, "Keep right in the middle of the road and win this silverfight." This was only the beginning: "After that we will get after the railroads, the telegraphs and the trusts." Its conclusion again affirms the radical character of fusion: "Let us get this free silver business disposed of and then the field will be cleared for action on the main principles of the populist party." [12]

A more grass-roots source, the Broken Bow, Nebraska, *Beacon*, presented fusion sentiment in a slightly different light, describing the tortuous course through which this policy often evolved. As early as March 1892 the *Beacon* insisted, "It is disgusting to think about this abominable fusion and it is hard to find language sufficiently strong to condemn it." Yet, by late 1895 the *Beacon* accepted fusion. It had, however, one reservation; fusion must develop along Populist lines, or not at all. Radicals, regardless of party, "must be united or the industrial forces are doomed to defeat, and the chances of emancipation from the thralldom of the money power rendered more precarious than ever." Either the reform forces would become "united and win, or remain separate and suffer defeat, as we have done in the past." One week later it asked, "Shall we as Populists eliminate the thousands who are with us against the Gold Standard, by setting up a creed?" No, "our motto should be—Go on with every reform, but concentrate all the forces for a decisive combat." In sum, it suggested in mid-December 1895, do not abandon "other important questions permanently," but remember "all prosperity is involved in the correct solution of the finance question." Then the *Beacon* vacillated, fearing it overstressed silver. "The campaigns from 1892 to the present time," it cautioned at the close of 1895, "have been fought on the Omaha platform." Hence, "The cardinal principles of that platform—finance, land and transportation, ought to be enacted into law." [13]

But the shift back was temporary; in the next issue,

and down to the election, the *Beacon* insisted that Populism could control the silver forces, and not the reverse. These forces were non-partisan, it argued, so "no one need sever his allegiance to his political party on entering its doors." Populism simply could not be swallowed up: "Afraid they'll capture the people's party. Oh no, no danger. We are 2,000,000 strong now. The chances are that there'll never be that many join the league." In fact, "If they do, more than half of them will get to be full fledged populists, and will find no objections whatever to all our demands." Its readers were less optimistic; one charged the paper two weeks later with compromising the platform out of existence: "As for our laying down the balance of our platform I say no. We have a vote of 2,000,000 who are solid for free silver and other reforms too, and we are not willing to lay down on these other issues." Instead, "Let's hold out the hand of brotherhood to the free silverites to come to us, but warn them in time that the only chance of success lies in their coming to us." The *Beacon* felt itself misunderstood; it countered that it "never said it was in favor of dropping a single plank of the Omaha platform. Not one." To support silver was not anti-radical: "We suggested that all join on the one dominant issue of financial reform, and then let a plank be adopted pledging the party if given power, to submit the transportation, the land question, the liquor question, etc., to a vote of the people." Hurt, it protested, "No one can possibly maintain for a moment that this is abandoning a demand of the Omaha platform." [14]

The controversy continued. Significantly, whatever the disagreement, readers questioned the paper's judgment but never its radicalism. One letter in mid-March inquired, "Are not the silvermen just as selfish as the goldmen? Can we expect or reasonably ask their support in favor of a legal tender paper currency or government banks after they secure the free coinage of silver?" Then it went to the heart of the matter: "Do you think for a moment they will assist us in carrying out any policy which will tend to make their silver money less valuable?" But the *Beacon* was not yet prepared to hear such criticism—at least, not for another month.[15]

Then, by late April, it too admitted "every good populist knows that the restoration of silver would not mean permanent relief." Now came the same argument previously ignored: "The power of a few to control the circulating medium would still remain where it is." Thus, the only solution "must be a thorough and radical change in the financial system." Otherwise, "the people will continue to suffer from panics with all their attendant evils." With the People's party convention two months off, it warned the Democrats not to "be fooled into thinking that populists will flock" to their party "in the event of free silver controlling the convention." In fact, "The democratic party has had its chance, failed, and it will be impossible to expect the people to trust them again." "Populists," it concluded, "have left the two old parties forever." But the *Beacon* did not oppose fusion; quite to the contrary, it wanted fusion, but on honorable terms—outside the major parties, and on a broader platform than silver. "Nearly all of them [Populists] are in favor of a union which will not involve the abandonment of principles, but there must be a common ground on which to unite, and that ground must be OUTSIDE THE CAMPS OF THE TWO OLD PARTIES." Yet, despite this stricture, the *Beacon* too fell in behind Bryan. No principles, it felt, had been sacrificed; the Democratic party had changed so drastically that it was no longer one of the "old" parties. Indeed, the roots of fusion ran deep. This paper, like many others, had thoroughly discussed the policy in the two years preceding the 1896 convention. No one had been surprised or tricked; by July 1896 the movement was ready to make a deliberate choice. Populism, while wrong, had not departed in a conservative direction.[16]

The Wahoo paper, staunchly anti-fusion until February 1896, is a final case in point. That month it announced the change by first placing its own radicalism beyond doubt: "It need not be more than mentioned that the *New Era*, or at least this present editor, has always been esteemed a radical adherent to the radical enunciations of the radical principles of the Omaha platform." But Populism must be realistic, for "it is not to be forgotten that political changes are accomplishable only by majorities." The moment had come to move toward larger objectives, but only by riding the present wave of financial agitation: "Great political issues are not created by platform declarations; they spring spontaneous from the public mind and when so presented are never settled until settled right." Accordingly, "The student of current events may detect a growing concentration of the public eye on one of the chief heads of monopoly, to wit: its manipulation of finance." This groundswell of discontent must be utilized to activate radicalism; but more, the financial question is in its own right a basic challenge worthy of the radical's notice. "The rehabilitation of silver, the abolition of banks of

issue, the issue by the government only of such paper
money as may be necessary and the creation of the postal
savings banks" will combine "millions of electors, who
have not affiliated with the party on its Omaha platform."
In the last analysis, fusion was for the radical a hope, a
gamble, and a necessary first step: "If the Populist party
can rise to the wisdom of seizing upon these issues, without loading itself with unaccomplishable declarations of
even good things, it will march with long strides toward
victory." [17]

Thus far, only the radicals have spoken: Fusion, despite conservative interference, was the opportunity to
create a larger, more radical Populism. But what of these
conservatives? Did they, as other Populists and later
historians believe, actually try to destroy the movement?
The views of James B. Weaver, People's party nominee
for president in 1892 and subsequently its leading fusion-
ist, reveal the conservative position in a highly different
light. For Weaver, fusion was entirely plausible and—
this is important—not at all a dilution of Populist radicalism. Fusion was surrounded by confusion; Weaver was
misunderstood within the party, for he saw what for two
years the radicals refused to see: There was a growing
cleavage in the Democratic party, chiefly in the midwest
and south, which was bringing the reform groups closer
together. In a word, he was ahead of his time, virtually
predicting the 1896 fusion when to do so was unpopular.

He wrote Bryan before the 1894 election, "Our people are making the mistake of their lives." Now was the
time for combining: "They do not seem to know there
has been an earthquake and that in consequence things
are shaken to pieces and broken into fragments." The

failure of fusion "will simply insure the return of the Rep party to power." Here Weaver went the more radical Populists one step better; whatever danger fusion posed to radicalism, a Republican victory would forestall all reform under the guise of a pseudo-reform movement. If the Republicans won, this meant "the passage of some half-hearted deceptive measures which will either kill of[f] the reform movement or retard it for a quarter of a century." Then, writing Bryan after the election, Weaver prophetically noted the coming split in the Democratic party, a split not wholly recognized by contemporaries until mid-1896: "It is now apparent that the Eastern and Western Democracy can never harmonize on current issues and that they must separate which will precipitate a new order of things." Then and there he gave frank warning of his future course; Weaver was no opportunist disguising his belief in fusion: "Let us be ready for it and help to shape things properly." [18]

Disturbed by "the result of the St. Louis conference," the maintenance of the Omaha platform, he confided to Ignatius Donnelly at the start of 1895: "I feel sure something must be done and done quickly to reassure public sentiment or the opportunity [to] settle the currency question—the great contention of the age—will pass away from our party during the present year and forever." Weaver's conservatism meant narrowing the platform to the financial question; it did not mean scrapping the platform. "We can no more settle the threefold contention of the Omaha platform in a single struggle than we could fight three battles at one and the same time with a single body of troops." He was conservative only by Populist standards.[19]

"Our mutual friends," Weaver warned Donnelly in March 1895, are placing us "at seeming cross purposes." This was unfair. "We are both working to the same end," he protested, "trying to get all the reform forces together on common ground, without fusion and outside the old parties." Thus, Weaver saw fusion not as the submergence of Populism into the Democratic party, but the uniting of all radical groups into a new party. Hence, "The *Nation* is passing into a whirlwind and the Populists must guide the storm." And to do this, Populism must concentrate on silver and recruit wherever possible: "I have found the study of the Free Soil platforms from 1840 to 1860 of great profit." Weaver had done his homework on displacing major parties. Three days later he again appealed to Donnelly, "Let us not fight these kindred factions spring up every where. Rather let us keep on such friendly relations with them that we can all agree in 1896 and save the country." And on the silver forces, "If our Bimetallic friends can aid us in smashing old party lines and in gathering into a common fold the vast multitude now outside our lives I bid them go ahead with this blessed work." This, then, is the rule-of-thumb to follow: "I feel like exclaiming as did a very great person on a similar occasion . . . 'Forbid them not. He who is not against us is for us.' " [20]

Weaver's stand in its final and most emphatic form was expressed in a confidential letter to Bryan, the last day of 1895: "We have had quite enough middle of the road nonsense, and some of us at last think it about time for the exhibition of a little synthetic force if we would accomplish any good purpose." He concluded, "The elements are now at hand out of which we certainly can construct an enduring and formidable force for the defense of popular rights." Then, with the Democratic convention several weeks away, he proposed to Bryan the following strategy: "Should the silver men be able to control the Chicago convention both as to platform and nominations be careful to have the platform cover the entire money question: second let your nominations be advisory simply and not final." Clearly, Weaver wanted so much more than free silver. He called for a new third force in American politics, one using the entire financial question as the springboard to major party status. Yet, perhaps I am too charitable; many Populists would have thought so.[21]

Davis Waite, former Populist governor of Colorado and one of the more outspoken radicals, complained to Donnelly in April 1895: Weaver "has greater confidence in the bi-metallic outfit than I have." But Waite questioned Weaver's judgment, not his sincerity or radicalism. "He thinks the new party really want the free coinage of silver at the ratio of 16 to 1 of gold, and abolition of banks of issue, their circulation to be supplied by greenbacks." Hence, even Waite conceded that Weaver did not favor a narrow definition of the financial question. In fact, as Waite further related, when he told Weaver "that the government legal tender clause was only bait to catch populist 'suckers,' and that the new party demand would simmer down to the single issue of silver," Weaver "swore by all the bald headed gods, that if that proved to be the case, he would drop the new party like a hot potatoe." Waite was more doubtful four months later, writing Donnelly: "Between you and me, I have not found Weaver entirely reliable, and his influence which was almost dominating in our party before he became mixed up in fusion matters, has always been against us in the fight I have been compelled to make in Colo." A more rank-and-file attack came from Little Sioux, Iowa, in mid-May 1896. The silver convention at St. Louis, it contended, "will be managed by Plutes to Bust up the Peoples Party," while the Democrats "will declare for free silver 16 to 1 and then vote the Republican ticket." As a result, "the Peoples Party will cast less votes this [election] than they did in 94." As for the culprit responsible, "Weaver killed all the hopes of the Party by his Fusion." [22]

Still, even though fusion proved disastrous, this cannot be blamed on Weaver. His own and the radical position were not that different at the moment of decision. Further, his view, as indeed fusion itself, becomes more plausible when the change in the Democratic party is noted. Bryan did not receive the Democratic nomination simply because he delivered the "Cross of Gold" speech; radical Democracy was not born on the convention floor.

Writing in the Omaha *World Herald*, Bryan gave a remarkable and radical blueprint for fusion as early as November 1894. "There are several questions," he began, "upon which the democrats and populists of the west and south are united." These included the tariff, income tax, and silver; it was on the last of these that he dwelt. But Bryan did not gloss over the differences between Democrats and Populists on this question. For example, "As to the question of paper money mutual concessions are necessary." There would also be some disagreement over banks of issue, for some opposed state and others national banks of issue. Here Bryan flatly stated: "The bank of issue is open to grave objections, whether it be a state bank or a national bank." In a word, Bryan regarded silver as only a part of the financial question, and was himself prepared to take a position about as advanced on the total problem as were the Populists. Thus, "No bank of issue can be established which does not confer a special and valuable privilege by law upon a favored individual or class of individuals."

The conflict over banks went deeper; at stake was control over the financial system itself: "Banking corporations, if given the power to determine the volume of currency, can fix the exchangeable value of the dollar and thus determine the value of all private property." Accordingly, he proposed, "Instead of declaring in favor of paper money issued by either state or national banks, we can agree upon a platform like this: 'We believe that the right to issue money is an attribute of sovereignty, and therefore favor the issue of all paper money needed by the federal government as the greenbacks were issued.' " The principle set down, Bryan continued: " 'We are in favor of making every dollar, whether it be gold, silver or paper, a full legal tender for all debts public or private . . .' " After touching upon further common ground, direct election of senators, Bryan entered the sensitive area of social control over corporations. Again, differences were reconcilable: While Democrats favor "regulation and control" to socialism, they "will prefer the government ownership of railroads to the railroad ownership of government if they have to choose between the two." Bryan's conclusion underscores the dramatic change in his party. "It will be easy, therefore, to agree upon the strict regulation and control of the railroads and other corporations by both federal and state governments within their respective spheres." [23]

Indeed, Bryan reflected the Democratic cleavage even earlier. The financial question already loomed large in May 1892 when he wrote Horace Boies, Democratic governor of Iowa: "On a financial question like this the rich and the poor are usually found on opposite sides for the obvious reason that their interests differ. When legislation is necessary, as it seems to me to be now, I do not hesitate to choose the side of the poor." Bryan sensed there was "a deep seated feeling, especially in the West and South, that our finances have been manipulated by the money centers and that the mass of people have suffered thereby." He readily admitted, "I fully share in this feeling." The regional distinction within the Democratic party was thus becoming a reality not in the summer of 1896 but four years earlier. And Bryan saw this as the start of a new movement: "A union of the democrats" in the west and south provides the entering wedge through which "the country can only be released from this pernicious control."

This was the crucial first step; intra-party fusion paved the way, although Bryan did not yet see this, for the larger fusion. But, for here and now, Cleveland's domination must be overthrown. The south and west are ready; there can be no delay: "What have we to gain by evasion or cowardice, in the North-East?" Boies, Bryan urged, must help challenge the financial policy of the eastern wing, a group closer to the Republicans than to radical Democrats. "These moneyed men know the record of our party and will not trust us as they do the Republicans. We cannot deceive them." Further, "They know that our party as a party favors coinage, that if any relief comes from the present financial system, it will come through the Democratic party." Hence, the party was coming to repudiate conservative leadership; positive action was now needed: "We will therefore gain nothing from them, and would, on the other hand discourage and drive away a large number of people who feel that something ought to be done, and would trust the Democracy if it gave a real promise of relief." Bryan concluded, "We do not need two republican parties, and when we begin to bid against the republican party for the eastern support we will enter a losing contest." [24]

Bryan was not a Populist; he did not even acknowledge the People's party nomination until the closing weeks of the campaign. Still, his views expressed a groundswell of discontent which even radical Populists could not ignore. Nor was he an opportunist. In 1893, when queried by the Postmaster-General on his political orthodoxy, Bryan replied: "In my own judgment, I am a democrat, simon-pure." But he hastened to add, in a manner not calculated to increase his patronage, "While I have regarded the name as peculiarly appropriate, I confess that I am more wedded to the principles than to the name, and if I were compelled to surrender the one or the other, I would stay with the principles and give up the name." Here, then, was the raw material for fusion—program taking priority over organization: "I have thus far acted with the democratic organization, because I believed it most capable of bringing to the people relief from the iniquitous legislation fastened upon them by the republican party, and I will not promise to give it allegiance after that belief is gone." [25]

Bryan did not speak in the wilderness; Populists, at

the time of his *World Herald* editorial, were already watching him closely. Ignatius Donnelly, writing Weaver in January 1895, already saw Bryan as a potential leader of the radical coalition. Donnelly, generally thought to be the most vocal anti-fusionist, asserted: *"The sensible men must husband their strength until the time comes, in 1896, to draw our platforms."* This was a call for fusion, but along Populist lines. Donnelly urged Weaver, "In the meantime you and Taubeneck are the men to confer with Bryan, Bland, etc. and arrange for a break up of the Democratic lines, with a Populist platform, and the doors open for cooperation with the People's Party." Thus, if Bryan could pass muster with Donnelly, it should come as no surprise that the fusion tide was rising.[26]

And why not? Bryan seemed more radical than he actually was, when placed beside conservative Democrats. The abuse heaped upon him by members of his own party could not but lessen Populist suspicions. This aspect of the Democratic cleavage, the increasing intransigeance on the right, added one more element to the plausibility of fusion. Gold Democrats had as great a hand in creating the Bryan image as any radical statement he could possibly make. One need only look at the correspondence of J. Sterling Morton, Cleveland's secretary of agriculture, and from Bryan's own state, to see what had happened in the Democratic party.

Morton warned the Nebraska governor in June 1896, "It seems now as though all the fanaticisms in finance were to be gathered under one flag. The massing of Populists, free-silver Democrats, and free-silver Republicans, and the old greenback cranks of long ago, under one flag and on one ticket now seems quite a terrible possibility." Here the outright denial of democratic principles crops through: This would be "a dangerous party in a country like ours where the elective franchise is the privilege of the ignorant and vicious as well as the enlightened and good." On the same day, to a London banker, Morton placed himself to the right of the Republicans as well: "The money fallacies in the United States are rampant and victorious, so far as the Democratic organization is concerned, and the virus extends itself to the rank and file of the Republican and into every nook and cranny of the political and social fabric of the country." He fully expected the forthcoming Democratic convention to be Populist in spirit. "The Convention at Chicago will utter a platform full of all the fallacies and vagaries of the Populists, and at last will be endorsed by all the organized isms in the United States." Morton was clearly worried. On that same date he wrote still another friend that even McKinley "has no convictions at all on the question of finance, and that while he stands upon an allegedly gold-standard platform, he would have stood upon a platform proclaiming the periwinkle currency of New Amsterdam sound money, or coon skins a proper circulating currency," if his party requested it.[27]

The Democratic convention itself confirmed gold Democratic fears. Congressman Seth W. Cobb complained to Morton, "This silver craze cannot be arrested. The dissatisfied, the unemployed, the tramps have joined the misguided farmers and laboring men and are following blind leaders." And a correspondent in Seward, Nebraska, cried out, "In all my life I never saw so much

of a danger in a political platform as now confronts us."
He continued, "I never saw one where Anarchy and
plunder croped out So Surely, as in the one upon which
our friend Bryan stands." Bryan and radical Democracy
must be stopped: "It behooves every patriotic cittizen
from every party, where floats the Star Spangled banner,
to rise in his manly dignity and rebuke and restrain the
Hidra headed Monster, by voice, by pen, and by vote." [28]

Clearly, Populists and radical Democrats had no
monopoly on the emotional outpourings of the 1890's.
"I know of nothing to disturb your peace," Charles W.
Dabney, assistant secretary of agriculture, informed
Morton, "besides this cunningly devised and powerfully
organized cabal of Silverites & demagogues who would
wreck the country's peace, prosperity & honor all for
private gain or political spoils." With the campaign
drawing to a close, Morton's response became more
strident. Radical workers supported Bryan, he observed
to a friend in Nebraska City, "not on financial grounds,
but because they desire to have strikes and riots uninter-
fered with by Federal authority." The next day Morton
wrote his son, "During this campaign Bryan and his
crowd have appealed to all that is mean in human nature." Thus, "There is no vicious characteristic of civi-
lized humanity that has not been aroused to hatred of
wealth, capital, and well-to-do people generally." Again
to his son, five days later, Morton carped on the injustice
of popular elections: "Never before have the theories of
self-government been menaced with so many disasters.
If Bryan and his crew can carry this country for their
vagaries, then our incapability for self-government is
proved." "Mules, swine and dogs," he added, "could be

taught the automatic vote, furnished with tickets and determine an election with just as much sense as many of those who wield the ballot power at the elections in the United States." [29]

With only days remaining until the election, Morton denounced Bryan, again to his son, in these terms: "In the white-heat frenzy which the proletariats have worked up under the leadership of Bryan—who, as a sort of Peter the Hermit, has proved himself to be a competent leader of the commune—there is nothing which happened during the French Revolutions and Communes" which cannot now happen here. This was the voice of conservative Democracy in Nebraska speaking; the party cleavage had become a veritable chasm. Morton concluded that "nothing which ever happened during the worst periods of any French Revolution would be impossible under the direful catastrophe of Bryan's election." And to another son he exclaimed, "There is great peril now in all of the populational centers of the United States. Tumults, riots, bloodshed and incendiarism are imminent." Finally, he stated to a friend in Omaha, "No human power can avert panic, calamity, political and social disruption, riot, bloodshed and anarchy, if the doctrines of the Chicago platform are to become the policy of this Republic." Then suddenly the cloud lifted. Morton pronounced in his election postmortem: "In my judgment, we have escaped the calamity of the commune." [30]

To juxtapose Bryan and Morton thus dramatizes the Democratic split; for many Populists fusion *was* plausible. The one obstacle to considering fusion radical as well—the Populist attitude toward silver—now merits a closer look. So far, the evidence clearly shows Populism was not fooled by this issue. More to the point, even Populists who emphasized silver did so entirely within a radical context.

Thus, Davis Waite, certainly a radical Populist, urged Donnelly in early 1894 that Populism must maintain exclusive rights over free silver: "The Omaha Platform is squarely for silver, and it is the only National Party that is." Only the enemies of Populism want silver to be "not a political question, but an economic question, to be supported, and finally procured inside the old party lines." Thus, silver was an entering wedge against the major parties—but silver as understood by Populists, not by those "professed friends of silver" who seek "to consider the silver question non-partizan." For Waite, then, silver was the first step to settling the financial question; although from Colorado, he pointed his remarks directly against the silver interests. Nor did support of silver necessarily imply the acceptance of fusion. By Waite's reasoning, if Populism retained control over the silver issue, fusion would be unnecessary. He wrote Lewelling in July 1894, "The people are already aroused as they were not at the last presidential campaign even at its close: The Miners, both silver & coal miners; the laborers and now the ranchmen are swarming over to the Populist party. There will be no fusion here with the democracy." Waite was strongly anti-fusionist at this time: "Am glad that you made no fusion with the democracy in Kansas." [31]

Waite opposed radical Democrats as late as December 1894. "The Sell out of the Dems to the Reps," he remarked to Donnelly, "was most infamous—and the sole

end in view was to destroy the populist party." Democrats supported silver only to steal the Populist thunder:
"They favored or claim that they do, the Populist plank
on Silver, *but do not favor any other plank in the populist platform.*" Yet, one year later, Waite beseeched
Bryan to bring radical Democrats into the Populist fold.
The Democratic party has betrayed the principles of
Jefferson; an old-line Democrat must now seek elsewhere: "There are now only three live Democratic
issues of the days of Jefferson and Jackson—to wit—the
war upon National and State Banks, the Income Tax and
the Free Coinage of Silver." None of these, Waite
asserted, had been endorsed by either major party.
"Upon all these issues both the old parties—the Republican on principle, the Democratic controlled by their
leaders and the administration are united on the Hamil-
tonian or AntiDemocratic Principle." Waite clearly
played on Bryan's sympathies; Populism alone was
"based upon the principles of true Democracy." Hence,
there must be fusion—but only on Populist terms: "I
have no confidence that the Democratic bolt on silver
will create a new Democratic Party but I believe the
Peoples Party can be made the embodiment of the principles of true Democracy." Waite unabashedly courted
Bryan; party labels were no longer important. "It is not
so much names as principles that we need." [32]

Thus, a leading radical Populist had shifted consider-
ably on fusion—from categorical rejection to qualified
acceptance. Then, on the eve of the People's party convention, Waite went the whole way: "I think that Mr.
Bryan is the only man that the reformers of this country
can decide on with hope of electing their choice. It is

the only and last chance the American people will have of settling the great financial question peaceably." Here again it becomes clear that radicals were not steamrolled on the convention floor. Waite summed up the new feeling toward the Democrats: Certainly, Populists "have been horribly abused," especially in the south, by the Democrats, but "I say it is unfair to hold Bryan, Altgeld and Pennoyer and such great reform men responsible for the sins and mistakes of the old party." [33]

Still, Waite proved the exception—not on fusion, but on silver. Populists, even when they did not flatly repudiate silver, were more lukewarm in regarding it a first step. Further evidence—letters to Donnelly's *Representative* in April 1895—underscores this point. One held that many silver advocates were "instruments of the great monopolies and corporations, which have brought the country to such ruin." Populists cannot be expected to follow "the lead of men who are known as corporation attorneys, and men of great wealth who seek to increase their wealth by means of mines, without sharing in the least with the feelings of the masses on other points." To do so, the letter concluded, was to presume "Populists are even greater asses than the party press has continually claimed them to be." Another letter insisted, "We have other causes of oppression that need redress as well as our monetary system." Hence, "our present railroad system and laws favorable to them, as well as our national banking system are as important a factor." And a third letter simply noted, "The People's Party is not a one plank party, but considers the government ownership of railroads and the national banking system as questions of equal importance." [34]

Nor are these isolated comments. The Topeka *Advocate* took this same position: "We hold to the declaration so often made before, that *any* settlement of the finance question that is unaccompanied by other changes, will be a disappointment; and we must insist upon the other changes that will render our financial measures effective." This was in January 1895; two months later, attacking the American Bimetallic League, it stated: Populism must "let the world know that we *are* a party and not a mere caudal appendage" of the silver interests. In fact, this "new bimetallic party is a mere bluff designed to secure a free coinage plank in the republican and democratic platforms in 1896." Elsewhere in this issue the *Advocate* chided those who, despite monopolistic abuses, "talk of curing our social and industrial ills simply by the free coinage of silver." Or as the Osceola, Nebraska, paper noted, "The Populist party was organized before the silver question was the main issue and the other issues upon which the party was founded are still important questions." For example, "No argument will convince the people of the west that the transportation question is not of great importance." And on the concentration of land ownership, "how can a real reform party defer consideration of a question involving the basic right of citizenship, viz: the right to a home, and spend its energies in the advocacy of free coinage alone?" This paper too endorsed fusion *before* the People's convention.[35]

Significantly, even Populists more receptive to the silver issue than the foregoing were still highly critical. "The money question," maintained a letter in the Broken Bow paper, "as understood by the rank and file of the people's party, is quite distinct from that advocated by the so-called silver or bi-metallic party." The difference was simple: "With the latter, the free and unlimited coinage of silver is the sole, vital issue before the country; while populists, not underrating the silver question, have always contended that full monetary relief can only come to the country from a comprehensive financial scheme." This was of course a direct slap at the silver literature. These pamphlets wanted only a quantitative increase in silver; they never mentioned the entire financial question, let alone other Populist demands. Populists, on the other hand, "insist upon a system of true scientific money, maintained permanently by the government, without dependence upon intermediary agencies of any kind whatever." [36]

Populism therefore never accepted free silver as a panacea. It simply could not; the movement was founded in such basic discontent that silver seemed only a hollow mockery of what Populism deemed necessary to remake America. A letter from Garnett, Kansas, to the Holdredge, Nebraska, paper expressed this feeling: "Populism was born of the dire necessities of the great common people. It voices the protest of millions against a long series of oppressions and usurpations." It "sprang from the so-called sub-stratum of our social fabric," and not from "the so-called higher classes." Since the latter are "favorites of fortune and recipients of countless unearned blessings, they desire no change." These higher classes "are above the terrible grasp of extreme necessity or the appalling sense of utter destitution that burns like a consuming fire into the very vitals of the suffering poor." What could silver offer to the radical born of

such oppression? "The Omaha platform," the letter mentioned, "evolved from such conditions. Its preamble
voises the dire extremity of millions who have suffered
till they feel and know." In this light, Populists necessarily asked searching questions on free silver: "Is such
coinage of more importance than the saving to the people
of $500,000,000 annually through government ownership
of telegraph, telephone, and express lines? Is it of greater
significance than the demand that the people own and
operate the trusts and not the trusts own and victimize
the people?" The road had been too hard; Populism
refused to settle for silver alone: "All these things have
the people demanded. All these reforms do they expect
from the hands of the young and vigorous party that
stands to-day as firmly for free coinage as for any other
tenet of its political faith." Hence, if fusion meant only
free silver, let there be no fusion: "Let there be no
trifling with things that are sacred. Let there be no barter
and sale of principles for temporary victory." [37]

Silver, then, was never more than a partial solution.
"Silver is only a part of the question," George F. Washburn, eastern division chairman of the party, wrote
Donnelly, "and no more important than a half dozen
other parts of it all of which are less important than the
question whether the banks or the government shall issue
our money and control it." This leads into a final point:
the focus on silver sometimes had a deeper significance.
The Broken Bow, Nebraska, paper saw silver as confirm-
ing the government's right to create monetary values.
Thus, the financial question asserted the principle of
government supremacy—first in one realm and then in
others. In the same breath the *Beacon* suggested, "Our

platform demands a complete change in the financial system; that the government shall take immediate possession of the railroads and telephones under the right of eminent domain." These "are two distinct issues presented to the people," and yet they are not unrelated. "The great question," it continued in this May 1896 editorial, "for solution at this time is, whether to hold in abeyance for the time being, the one of less importance until the other is settled in the interest of the whole people. This is a question upon which honest populists differ." The paper believed finance should come first, for this was a step in the direction of government ownership: "Let money be made the first plank, and then declare that the government shall take charge of the Union Pacific system of roads, so as to test the feasibility of government ownership." Hence, "Such a plank would strengthen the one in regard to money and in that way, government ownership could be approached gradually." Even Populists who advocated silver had not sacrificed radical principles. Here the financial question was more than an expedient; it was an assertion of Populist radicalism.[38]

That much is now clear; fusion *was* intended as a radical policy. Beside isolated socialists, only Lloyd and his circle thought otherwise—or at least thought that Populist leaders, while not opportunistic, were far less radical than the rank-and-file. Yet, even they do not indict the movement but only some of its leaders. As early as December 1893 Lloyd sensed, "Once again in history the people are ripening faster than their leaders." One year later he charged that, in the face of growing conservative militancy, "some of our leaders on the contrary appear determined to take narrower ground and throw the radicals in the party over-board." For Lloyd leadership was a decisive factor; the radical potential of Populism was in danger of being stifled. "Revolutions never go backward. If the People's Party goes backward it is not a revolution, and if it is not a revolution it is nothing." This was December 1894, a crucial time in Populist history, when the movement's electoral peak had been reached—and the farmer-labor coalition was crumbling. Hence, any sign of weakness on the part of the leadership would be acutely felt.[39]

"There will be an effort made at St. Louis," George H. Gibson informed Lloyd, "to eliminate, or shelve, the socialistic planks in our party and to recommend as leaders that we make free silver and government paper money—simply paid out—the issue, or the dominant question, with us." Another correspondent complained that this party conference was called "for the avowed purpose of eliminating everything from the Omaha platform save the financial demands." And still a third warned that H. E. Taubeneck, the People's party national chairman, and Weaver sought to "discard the Omaha planks and platform altogether." Further, they "spoke of the 'crank anarchists and socialists' in the party, and that they must be gotten rid of, and a 'June silver' party organized at once." Significantly, all efforts to undermine the radical principles failed. Here one cannot help but feel that these fears, even if correct, explain little about what was happening. Lloyd himself recognized that fusion would have resulted with or without the conservative leaders. Yet, much of his correspondence from this time on inflated the role of a handful of leaders.[40]

In May 1896 Henry R. Legate, a Massachusetts Populist and Nationalist leader, wanted radicals to "make a fight for our principles at St. Louis, for the simple reason that to do otherwise would look cowardly, and when we are beaten earnestly and vigorously protest against the narrowness of the platform and the abandonment of fundamental principles for a policy of expediency." That is, Legate was strongly anti-fusionist. Yet, despite his criticisms of Populist leadership, he too supported fusion only a few weeks later. Free silver, he wrote Lloyd in June, had to be settled before more radical measures were even possible: "The true reform movement of the future must be along socialistic or nationalistic lines, and the quicker the silver question ceases to be an issue the better, and am delighted at the prospect of the battle between gold and silver in the coming election." Silver, then, may have been a risk but it was a step in the right direction. "The free-silver fal-do-rol," observed A. B. Adair of the Chicago *Record*, "is playing havoc with the reform movement just at present, but that will exhaust itself in time, and then there will be a chance to work." [41]

When the People's party convention was less than two weeks away, Lloyd offered his most scathing indictment of the leadership. Stating that his "own preference for a ticket would be Coxey and Debs," he asked: "How can you get the delegates whom Taubeneck and his associates have been slumming for to support such men?" But Taubeneck was not malicious: "The simple truth is Taubeneck has been flim-flammed. The politicians at Washington got hold of him, persuaded him that 'free Silver' was the supreme issue." Hence, Democratic and silver politicians used him "to turn all the party maneuvres into building up this silver issue." Lloyd charged, then, not opportunism but stupidity; outside politicians created a diversion in order to sidetrack Populist demands and "pocket the whole thing for themselves." But this was not a crucial factor in fusion; in reality, the Democratic convention left Populism "only the Hobson's choice of sinking ourselves out of sight and resurection in the Democracy; or, of beginning, de novo within a few weeks of election, the task of making an issue and finding followers." An even deeper reason for fusion, however, lay with Populism itself. Despite its own skepticism on silver, Populism did make the issue well known. Thus, "The masses have been taught by us that 'silver' is the *issue*, and they will of course have the commonsense to give their votes to the most powerful of the parties promising it." Then came an interesting twist: Populist leaders were not too professional but too amateurish; they bungled the situation badly. Had Populism, Lloyd continued, "been in the hands of really practical politicians, instead of 'Glaubenichts' like Taubeneck, the full Omaha Platform could easily have been made the issue that would have held us together for a brilliant campaign, but now that cannot be done." Lloyd, on the eve of fusion, clearly saw the dilemma: "If we fuse, we are sunk; if we don't fuse, all the silver men we have will leave us for the more powerful Democrats." Still, whether or not fusion was necessary, Lloyd would not absolve the leaders from responsibility: "Curious that the new party, the Reform party, the People's Party should be more boss-ridden, ring-ruled, gang-gangrened than the two old parties of monopoly." [42]

Yet, there were mixed reactions to fusion even in the

Lloyd group. Bayard Holmes wrote the next day, "Bryan is a man whom I have known for two years and he is a true socialist at heart and in his beliefs, but he has not gone so far as to separate himself from the great parties." Lloyd was unconvinced. He replied to Holmes two days later, attacking not Bryan but the Populist leaders: "The men in the management of the P.P. who are specially and bitterly and traiterously opposed to the real issues now before the public are the ones who have fanned this free silver back fire." They played into the hands of the "railroad, telegraph, telephone, trust, bank and other monopolists," who want the people "beguiled into believing that *the* principal cause of their woes was that the privilege of the silver owners to compel the people to accept their product as legal tender had been taken away." Here, then, was the reasoning behind the famous "cow-bird" statement; monopolists encouraged silver agitation to obscure more basic grievances.[43]

In August, the convention over, another of Lloyd's correspondents dissented. Displeased initially with fusion, he now felt the course had radical possibilities: "But we have only the beginning now. It is a wholesome symptom —the wonderful revolution in the Democratic party; how the masses have really expressed their will and revolted from the domination of their plutocratic leaders." The writer added, "It is a great step in the impending revolution. Whatever the outcome the change will be accelerated." In fact, "If Bryan is elected we may expect to see a strong movement for government ownership of railways and telegraphs." But by this time Lloyd was thoroughly demoralized. "The philosophy of this People's Party disaster," he wrote in early August, "I take to be this: The leaders have never been men well grounded in reform principles, nor really desirous of effecting fundamental social and industrial changes." Rather, "They went so far and only so far with their platform as the pressure from the people compelled, and they were forever only too happy to respond to the voice of any siren of Fusion and slip out of the straight and narrow way of principle. . ." He had good cause to be bitter; standing almost alone, Lloyd accurately saw the final outcome. "The arrogance of the Democrats, the discouragement of the masses of the P.P., the practical difficulties of maintaining an organization whose leaders have all deserted, the schism between the radical and the opportunists—all these will increase daily." And this was only August. [44]

Lloyd came full circle in October 1896, denying all that he had said in the years of agitation. "The People's Party," he exclaimed to A. B. Adair, "is a fortuitous collection of the dissatisfied. If it had been organized around a clear-cut *principle* . . . it could never have been seduced into fusion, nor induced even to consider the nomination of a man like Bryan who rejects its bottom doctrine." This was followed by his blistering indictment of silver: "The Free Silver movement is a fake. Free Silver is the cow-bird of the Reform movement." The trick had worked; Populist radicalism had been successfully stopped: "It [free silver] waited until the nest had been built by the sacrifices and labor of others, and then it laid its eggs in it, pushing out the others which lie smashed on the ground. It is flying around while we are expected to do the incubating." But not Lloyd; he resigned from Populism. "I for one decline to sit on the nest to help any such game." He closed, "The People's Party has been betrayed, and all that, but after all it is its own fault. No party that does not lead its leaders will ever succeed." Lloyd voted for the Socialist Labor candidate.[45]

But this was not a fitting epitaph. Populism was not deceived on silver; it remained radical to the end. To conclude, one central point springs out from the evidence: Populism was a progressive social force. It accepted industrial society, posed solutions not seeking to turn back the clock, and was strongly pro-labor. Yet, the movement was progressive in a still more profound sense. Not only did Populism look forward rather than backward, but it also was deeply committed to freedom. It attacked the very character of industrial capitalist society, not only on economic but also humanistic grounds. Its critique was neither partial nor superficial; higher crop prices and lower interest rates were not the answer. The issue at stake was nothing less than human dignity. And for Populism this permitted but one conclusion: Industrial America must be altered in a truly democratic direction. Technology must be harnessed for human uses, not for creating the surplus worker. Indeed, Populism was more than a protest movement; it was a glorious chapter in the eternal struggle for human rights. Modern America might well profit from the Populist experience.

Sources

This is not a bibliography; for that see the excellent compilation in John D. Hicks, *The Populist Revolt* (Minneapolis, 1931). Only one major study on midwestern Populism has appeared in the intervening time, Chester McArthur Destler, *American Radicalism, 1865–1901* (New London, 1946); yet, more works are now promised, inspired largely by Richard Hofstadter's provocative essay in *The Age of Reform* (New York, 1955). Instead, I will discuss the primary sources making up the present book. Not that the monographic literature of the 1920's should be ignored; on the contrary, it contains the basic facts of political and economic history. But it unmistakably fails to tap the raw data of Populist ideology. As noted earlier, fully nine-tenths of the present evidence has not appeared before—even though perfectly accessible to the researcher. Hence, this note is intended as a guide, enabling others to benefit from my own trial-and-error approach.

Manuscripts. The Ignatius Donnelly Papers, Minnesota Historical Society, are the most important manuscript collection on midwestern Populism. Here the variety is extraordinary; there are not only correspondence between Donnelly and such national leaders as

Weaver, Waite and Bryan, but also by far the most representative statements in any set of holdings. It is the latter, the penciled yearnings of unlettered farmers, which had been altogether neglected. There is little else, however, in the way of helpful manuscripts at Minnesota. Neither those somewhat favorable to Populism (Charles W. Brandborg and Edwin H. Atwood Papers), nor those opposing the movement (Knute Nelson, James A. Tawney, Frank Austin Carle, and Solomon Comstock Papers), contain enough relevant information to warrant extensive researching.

The Henry D. Lloyd Papers, State Historical Society of Wisconsin, are the next most important collection. In fact, they directly complement the Donnelly Papers, the two together comprising the rural and urban dimensions of Populism. One sees in the Lloyd Papers aspects of Populism not found elsewhere, particularly the movement's relation to socialism, labor, and other radical currents. Also, because Lloyd and his correspondents were more concerned with national and even philosophic issues than was Populism as a whole, penetrating criticisms occur having value beyond their use as evidence. Truly disappointing, but worth the inspection, are the Luhman H. Weller and Robert Schilling Papers. For a critique of Populism from the left, the Socialist Labor Party and De Leon Papers are invaluable and deserve careful study. With the possible exception of the Richard T. Ely Papers, there is little to be found in the remaining collections at Wisconsin, whether in the papers of supporters or critics. These collections include the papers of Robert M. LaFollette, William F. Vilas, Jeremiah M.

Rusk, Nils P. Haugen, Thomas C. Richmond, William Toole, and Elisha W. Keyes.

The William V. Allen, Samuel Maxwell, and Samuel M. Chapman Papers, Nebraska State Historical Society, proved surprisingly inadequate. And the J. Sterling Morton Papers, while an excellent collection, had little relevance for the topic. A virtual mine of information, in part because it seemed untouched for decades, was the Nebraska State Farmers' Alliance Records. Here was an even more grass-roots source than the Donnelly Papers.

Moving next to the Iowa Department of History and Archives, I regret to say that the James B. Weaver Papers are scanty and unrewarding. (My own brief reconstruction of Weaver's views came from his letters in other collections.) The William Jennings Bryan Papers, Library of Congress, are another significant source, both on radical Democracy and Populism. Perhaps the best portion centers on the week immediately following the 1896 election. Here Bryan was deluged with letters often reflecting Populist views. These letters also mention with great frequency the degree of coercion used by Republicans during the campaign.

A final collection remains—the Lorenzo D. Lewelling Papers, Kansas State Historical Society. This holding proved the greatest surprise, for it appears not to have been previously used. In fact, the letters were for the most part contained in the series, *Governors' Letter-books*, CVIII–CX, or in folders organized by topic. These last are superb in revealing contemporary conditions. Also, there are several interesting items in the

Farmers' Alliance minutes of Gove county, Kansas. The foregoing summary in no way exhausts the possibilities; I was not able to research Populist manuscripts in such state historical societies as North and South Dakota, Colorado, and Illinois.

Newspapers. The collection in the Nebraska State Historical Society is excellent. With the Lincoln *Farmers' Alliance* as the proper starting place, one can then work exhaustively on the county level. The present work traces the county press in the seven strongest Populist areas, thus quite possibly biasing the evidence in a radical direction. If true, there is ample opportunity to restore the balance, for numerous other examples of the local press are in existence. In any case, I relied most heavily on the *Custer County Beacon* (Broken Bow), *Platte County Argus* (Columbus), and *Saunders County New Era* (Wahoo). In Minnesota, Donnelly's paper, the St. Paul *Representative*, is significant on two counts: It serves, through editorials, as his sounding board, and it contains a good cross-section of both urban and rural Populism in the letters column. *The People*, Socialist Labor Party organ, in numerous libraries, is basic for viewing the relation of Populism and socialism. Finally, I found the Topeka *Advocate*, Kansas State Historical Society, to be extremely valuable. Its editorials, unusually comprehensive and literate, discussed questions such as the role of technology in capitalist development and the significance of industrial violence. Kansas also has a fine newspaper collection, enabling the student to work on the county level, as in Nebraska.

Miscellaneous. The Donnelly and Lloyd Papers contain excellent scrapbooks, especially of newspaper clippings. There are also William V. Allen and William Jennings Bryan scrapbooks in Nebraska, and those belonging to John Davis in Kansas. Good pamphlet collections exist in the University of Nebraska and Kansas State Historical Society libraries. The first is concerned with Populist and non-Populist discussions of the financial question, and the second with specifically Populist political tracts. Also important are the unpublished theses done in the mid-1920's under Professor Buck's direction at Minnesota and in the late 1920's under Professor Hicks at Nebraska. These may be found either in the historical society or university libraries. But again it must be stressed that only the surface has been broken. Imagination and perseverance can uncover a great deal more on the grass-roots level.

I am deeply grateful to Frank Freidel and Louis Hartz for having read this book in manuscript, to the staffs of the state historical societies visited, and to my wife, Nancy, who aided me every step of the way. With Nannie beside me, this book was truly a labor of love.

Notes

ABBREVIATIONS

KSHS: Kansas State Historical Society
LC: Library of Congress
MHS: Minnesota Historical Society
NHS: Nebraska State Historical Society
WHS: State Historical Society of Wisconsin

INTRODUCTION

1. John D. Hicks, *The Populist Revolt* (Minneapolis, 1931), p. 237.

2. Solon J. Buck, *The Granger Movement* (Cambridge, 1913), pp. 310–312, and *passim*.

3. Hicks, pp. 412–413.

4. Chester McArthur Destler, *American Radicalism, 1865–1901* (New London, 1946), esp. chaps. i, vii–xi.

5. See C. Vann Woodward, "The Populist Heritage and the Intellectual," *American Scholar* (Winter 1959–60) for a critique of these developments.

CHAPTER ONE

". . . the fullness of the divinity of humanity."

1. Quoted in *Times* (Chicago), Nov. 4, 1894.

2. Hamlin Garland to James B. Weaver, July 23, 1892, Weaver Papers, Iowa Department of History and Archives; Ignatius Donnelly, printed address, September 1896, Donnelly Papers, MHS; William V. Allen, pamphlet of speeches (Washington, 1898), Allen Papers, NHS.

3. Lorenzo D. Lewelling, speech on July 28, 1894, KSHS; *Custer County Beacon* (Broken Bow, Neb.), Jan. 23, 1896, and *Nuckolls County Herald* (Nelson, Neb.), Oct. 30, 1896, both in NHS.

4. *Farmers' Alliance* (Lincoln, Neb.), Oct. 22, 1891, NHS.

5. Quoted in *Times* (Chicago), Nov. 4, 1894; *Platte County Argus* (Columbus, Neb.), Oct. 15, 1896, and *Saunders County New Era* (Wahoo, Neb.), July 23, 1896, both in NHS; Thomas C. Hall to Henry D. Lloyd, May 23, 1896, Lloyd Papers, WHS. At this time Darrow was active in the movement; for his subsequent reservations, however, see Chapter Five at note 17.

6. *Platte County Argus* (Columbus, Neb.), June 4, 1896, NHS.

7. Quoted in *Advocate* (Topeka, Kan.), Sept. 19, 1894, KSHS. Cf. this with Simon Sterne to Lloyd, Sept. 19, 1895, Lloyd Papers, WHS, for the difference between Populist and strongly liberal views on corporate practices regarding technology. Sterne, an eastern leader in the movement to regulate railroad rates, conceded that corporations "buy up new inventions and then consider whether it is wiser to smother or develop them." Yet, this does not arise "from the organization of trusts or from any monopolistic element." Here the gap is even wider; Sterne concludes, "It is the mere power of capital, and nothing more, and an attack upon this power strikes me as a little dangerous."

8. Lorenzo D. Lewelling, speech on July 28, 1894, KSHS; W. A. M'Keighan, "Wealth as a Political Power," *Farmers' Alliance* (Lincoln, Neb.), Apr. 14, 1890, NHS. See Irvin G. Wyllie, *The Self-Made Man in America* (New Brunswick, 1954) for an excellent analysis of the success myth.

9. *Farmers' Alliance* (Lincoln, Neb.), Feb. 28, 1891, and *Alliance-Independent* (Lincoln, Neb.), Feb. 1, 1894, both in NHS; *Advocate* (Topeka, Kan.), Sept. 20, 1893, KSHS. The *Alliance-Independent* added, "The only possible permanent democracy is the democracy of unselfish socialism."

10. Lorenzo D. Lewelling, speech on July 28, 1894, KSHS.

11. George H. Gibson to the editor, *Alliance-Independent* (Lincoln, Neb.), Apr. 27, 1893, NHS; Gibson to Lloyd, Dec. 6, 1895, Lloyd Papers, WHS.

12. J. N. Byington to Donnelly, Sept. 18, 1893, and Donnelly, printed address, September 1896, both in Donnelly Papers, MHS; *Platte County Argus* (Columbus, Neb.), Oct. 15, 1896, NHS.

13. Lloyd to Rev. B. Fay Mills, May 21, 1896, and Lloyd to Samuel Bowles, July 11, 1892, both in Lloyd Papers, WHS.

14. R. M. Probstfield to Donnelly, May 26, 1896, Donnelly Papers, MHS.

15. Alba Satterthuaite to Bryan, Nov. 8, 1896, Bryan Papers, LC; Donnelly, printed address, September 1896, Donnelly Papers, MHS.

CHAPTER TWO

Tramps and Vagabonds: Signs of the Time

1. *Farmers' Alliance* (Lincoln, Neb.), May 7, 1891, NHS. See Fritz Pappenheim, *The Alienation of Modern Man* (New York, 1959) for a superb discussion of alienation in present-day industrial society.

2. *Farmers' Alliance* (Lincoln, Neb.), Sept. 6, 1890, NHS.

3. *Ibid.*, Aug. 21, 1889, Mar. 3, 1892. The first concluded, "Therefore, be not deceived if something should be done by the coming congress for our relief . . . as it will only be a sup, a morsel to quiet us." The *Advocate* (Topeka, Kan.), Aug. 31, 1892, also criticized a society "which existing political parties . . . manifest no disposition to remedy."

4. Lloyd to Samuel Gompers, July 15, 1892, Lloyd Papers, WHS.

5. *Farmers' Alliance*, Mar. 3, Jan. 21, 1892, NHS.

6. *Alliance-Independent* (Lincoln, Neb.), Jan. 11, 1894, and *Farmers' Alliance* (Lincoln, Neb.), Mar. 10, 1892, both in NHS.

7. *Advocate* (Topeka, Kan.), Apr. 11, 1894, KSHS.

8. *Ibid.*, Apr. 10, 1895.

9. Clarence S. Darrow to Lloyd, Nov. 22, 1894, Lloyd Papers, WHS. Herbert Marcuse, in the *American Historical Review*, 54:558 (April 1949), persuasively argues for the same general standard. By focusing on a society's worst features, Marcuse notes in defense of Lord Acton's approach, one can "uncover the deepest layer of the whole system, the structure which holds it together, the essential condition for the efficiency of its political and economic organization."

10. Lorenzo D. Lewelling, executive proclamation issued Dec. 4, 1893, and reprinted in *Daily Capital* (Topeka, Kan.), Dec. 5, 1893, KSHS.

11. *Locomotive Firemen's Magazine* (Feb. 1894); *Advocate*

(Topeka, Kan.), Dec. 6, 27, 1893, KSHS. In the latter issue, the *Advocate* queried: "Shall the fear of 'paternalism' prevent interference with the system which has caused these conditions? Can government only provide work and food for men after they become criminals?"

12. J. A. Huffman to Lewelling, Dec. 6, 1893, and G. H. Fish to Lewelling, Dec. 9, 1893, both in Lewelling Papers, KSHS.

13. I. W. Canfield to Lewelling, Dec. 6, 1893, H. M. Greene to Lewelling, Dec. 5, 1893, Emmett Tiffany to Lewelling, Dec. 5, 1893, W. H. Sears to Lewelling, Dec. 7, 1893, James H. Lathrop to Lewelling, Jan. 1, 1894, Ella Ornsby to Lewelling, [n.d.], Frank Dibert to Lewelling, Dec. 21, 1893, H. H. Strand, with resolution enclosed, to Lewelling, Dec. 12, 1893, Brainerd, Minnesota Local, International Association of Machinists to Lewelling, Jan. 1, 1894, and Cincinnati, Ohio central labor council to Lewelling, Dec. 11, 1893, all in Lewelling Papers, KSHS.

14. Albert S. Frost to Lewelling, Dec. 5, 1893, and Andrew Jackson to Lewelling, Dec. 5, 1893, both in Lewelling Papers, KSHS.

15. R. L. Robinson to Lewelling, Dec. 5, 1893, Lewelling Papers, KSHS. I am reminded here of the fate of refugees in modern times. Pappenheim, pp. 45–46, quotes from Stefan Zweig's memoirs: "Human beings were made to feel that they were objects and not subjects, that nothing was their right but everything merely a favor by official grace." See also Mrs. F. V. Curns to Lewelling, Dec. 20, 1893, Lewelling Papers, KSHS, for what forced vagabondage meant in human terms. An Arizona woman recently dispossessed from the land, she exclaimed: "God only knows how the poor are being oppressed, all over the United States and scarcely any one in power to help them." "My story," she went on, "is the same as many thousands Mortgages with the fall in prices forced us out of Kansas to this new country." Yet, it is the realm of ordinary problems which best dramatizes the condition of this woman's life: "And here it takes the united effort of the whole family to make a bare living clothes is out of the question, so I have to make over old ones."

16. Lester C. Hubbard, printed address, August 1891, Luhman H. Weller Papers, WHS; Bayard Holmes to Lloyd, Oct. 24, 1894, Lloyd Papers, WHS.

17. Lloyd to W. T. Stead, Aug. 21, 1894, Lloyd Papers, WHS.

18. J. W. Sherwood to editor, *Farmers' Alliance and Nebraska Independent* (Lincoln, Neb.), Apr. 14, 1892, and *Alliance-*

Independent (Lincoln, Neb.), Mar. 1, 1894, both in NHS; *Advocate* (Topeka, Kan.), Oct. 31, 1894, KSHS. James B. Weaver, presidential candidate of the People's party in 1892, opposed in Congress (*Congressional Record*, 2nd Session, 49th Congress, 2701) the construction of armories as early as 1887: "And I warn this House, in the name of the laboring men of this country, not to pass legislation which looks to overawing the people by military establishments, but to go to work and undo the legislation which has brought about our present discontent."

19. B. O. Flower to Luhman H. Weller, June 13, 1894, Weller Papers, WHS.

CHAPTER THREE

The Farmer and Working Class Discontent

1. L. S. Orcutt to editor, *Alliance* (Lincoln, Neb.), Aug. 21, 1889, *Alliance-Independent* (Lincoln, Neb.), Aug. 11, 1892, and John Dudek, secretary of Union Alliance No. 1537, quoted in *Farmers' Alliance* (Lincoln, Neb.), Feb. 14, 1891, all in NHS.

2. Lester C. Hubbard to Lloyd, Aug. 18, 1890, Lloyd Papers, WHS; *Alliance* (Lincoln, Neb.), July 24, 1889, NHS; Minnesota state Farmers' Alliance declaration, Feb. 25, 1886, Edwin H. Atwood Papers, MHS; *Farmers' Alliance and Nebraska Independent* (Lincoln, Neb.), Apr. 7, 1892, NHS.

3. J. H. Powers to editor, *Alliance* (Lincoln, Neb.), Sept. 4, 1889, *Farmers' Alliance* (Lincoln, Neb.), July 19, Sept. 6, 1890, J. M. C. to editor, *Farmers' Alliance*, Mar. 21, 1891, all in NHS.

4. W. H. Bennington to editor, *Advocate* (Topeka, Kan.), Aug. 10, 1892, KSHS.

5. *Farmers' Alliance* (Lincoln, Neb.), Aug. 23, 1890, and *Alliance-Independent* (Lincoln, Neb.), July 14, 28, 1892, both in NHS.

6. *Advocate* (Topeka, Kan.), July 20, 1892, KSHS; Mary E. Lease to the editor, *ibid.*, July 27, 1892.

7. J. R. Detwiler to editor, *Advocate* (Topeka, Kan.), Aug. 3, 1892, KSHS; Mitchell county Alliance resolution in *ibid.*, July 27, 1892. Comparing Populist views on Homestead with those of the country at large, one sees clearly the radical character of Populism. J. Bernard Hogg, *The Homestead Strike of 1892* (unpublished Ph.D. dissertation, University of Chicago, 1943), pp.

143–193, concludes, after an intensive analysis of newspapers and public statements, that opinion was "all of a like purpose; to solidify capital in its right to manage its property as it saw fit, without restraint from anyone, least of all from labor."

8. Interview with Lewelling, *Advocate* (Topeka, Kan.), Apr. 25, 1894, KSHS; *ibid.*, Apr. 11, 1894.

9. *Ibid.*, Apr. 25, May 2, 1894, Feb. 6, 1895.

10. Resolution of Oak Valley Alliance, May 5, 1894, and resolution of Burt county Alliance, June 9, 1894, both in *Nebraska State Farmers' Alliance Records*, NHS.

11. H. F. Wasmund to Luna E. Kellie, May 14, 1894, A. L. Pennington to Kellie, May 2, 1894, and Ella Whitman to Kellie, May 7, 1894, all in *Nebraska State Farmers' Alliance Records*, NHS; *Polk County Independent* (Osceola, Neb.), Aug. 22, 1895, NHS.

12. William V. Allen, speech on Apr. 19, 1894 (pamphlet), and *Morning Journal* (New York), Apr. 29, 1894, in Scrapbook, 1893–96, both in Allen Papers, NHS; *Wealth Makers* (Lincoln, Neb.), Apr. 5, 1894, NHS; H. E. Taubeneck to Donnelly, Mar. 12, Apr. 27, 1894, Donnelly Papers, MHS. See *Advocate* (Topeka, Kans.), May 16, 1894, KSHS, for one Populist solution to the industrial army question—a vast public works program. Annie L. Diggs urged John Davis to introduce an Industrial Army Bill in Congress, empowering the secretary of war "to enlist, as fast as practicable, five hundred thousand men in an industrial volunteer army." They would "be employed on works of public improvements, such as canals, rivers, and harbors, irrigation works, public highways, and other such public improvements as congress . . . shall provide."

13. Speeches by Davis Waite and Annie L. Diggs quoted in *State Journal* (Topeka, Kans.), July 13, 1894, KSHS; John S. McFadden, secretary, A.R.U. local 48, to Lewelling, July 4, 1894, and William Tanner, secretary, trades assembly of Kansas City, Kans., to Lewelling, July 9, 1894, both in Lewelling Papers, KSHS.

14. W. M. Goodnes to Lewelling, July 4, 1894, W. H. Hamm to Lewelling, July 14, 1894, and Charles W. Marsh to Lewelling, June 30, 1894, all in Lewelling Papers, KSHS.

15. *Wealth Makers* (Lincoln, Neb.), July 5, 26, 1894, NHS. The paper reported on July 14, 1894, "The executive committee of the National Farmers Alliance and Industrial Union . . . passed strong resolutions of sympathy for the American Railway Union

strikers and agreed to open the granaries and warehouses to A.R.U. and K. of L. to assist them to stand out for their just demands."

16. *Advocate* (Topeka, Kan.), July 18, 25, Sept. 19, 1894, KSHS.

17. John Davis, "Danger of the Times," written July 1894 and reprinted in *Railway Times*, Feb. 15, 1895, John Davis Scrapbooks, KSHS.

18. *Advocate* (Topeka, Kan.), Jan. 16, 1895, KSHS; Governor's Message of 1895, quoted in *ibid.*, Jan. 9, 1895. That Lewelling singled out these two counties suggests an important point: Industrial labor was often found in primarily agrarian states. Thus, there was ample opportunity for farmers and workers to develop mutual interests. Both counties, coal-mining areas, gave disproportionately higher votes to Populist candidates. Weaver received a bare majority of the total Kansas vote in the 1892 presidential election, but was given 57 per cent in both Cherokee and Crawford counties; in 1896 the state vote for Bryan was 51 per cent, while it was 58 per cent in Cherokee and 54 per cent in Crawford. See W. Dean Burnham, *Presidential Ballots, 1836–1892* (Baltimore, 1955), pp. 435–439; Edgar Eugene Robinson, *The Presidential Vote, 1896–1932* (Stanford University Press, 1934), pp. 200–202.

19. *Alliance-Independent* (Lincoln, Neb.), Jan. 18, 1894, *Custer County Beacon* (Broken Bow, Neb.), Aug. 22, Nov. 21, 1895, *Saunders County New Era* (Wahoo, Neb.), Feb. 20, May 21, 1896, and *Beacon Light* (O'Neill, Neb.), [n.d. but probably April 1896], in Allen Scrapbooks, 1893–96, all in NHS.

20. *Farmers' Alliance* (Lincoln, Neb.), Aug. 30, 1890, NHS.

21. *Advocate* (Topeka, Kan.), Oct. 26, 1892, Jan. 30, 1895, KSHS. See *Populist Party Clippings*, I, KSHS, for Kansas People's party resolutions in 1892. Quoted from the *Topeka Mail* (Topeka, Kan.), June 24, 1892, one resolution commended Populist state representatives for "the passage of the bill making the Pinkerton detective system amenable to law, also the bill abolishing the blacklisting and discharging employes without an opportunity to be heard in their defense." Significantly, another stated that "although the people's party of Kansas is largely composed of farmers, we sympathize with all classes of laborers and will aid them in their contest for a better system and a more equitable division of the profits of their toil, and we invite their co-operation in our warfare against a common enemy."

22. *Saunders County New Era* (Wahoo, Neb.), July 9, 1896, and *Custer County Beacon* (Broken Bow, Neb.), Nov. 7, 1895, both in NHS; Lewelling to Frank P. McLannan, July 26, 1893, *Governors' Letterbooks,* CIX, KSHS.

23. John B. Thomson to Donnelly, June 30, 1892, Donnelly Papers, MHS; *Advocate* (Topeka, Kan.), Feb. 7, 21, 1894, KSHS.

24. *Ibid.,* Mar. 20, July 3, 1895, KSHS.

25. Ethelbert Stewart to Lloyd, Oct. 12, 1894, Lloyd Papers, WHS.

26. Resolution of Gove county Alliance, Apr. 18, 1891, *Farmers' Alliance Minutes,* KSHS.

27. John B. Lennon to Gompers, July 20, 1896, quoted in Philip S. Foner, *History of the Labor Movement in the United States* (New York, 1955), II, 338. See Destler, pp. 234-236, for the impact of Gompers' stand at Denver on the farmer-labor alliance in Chicago. *American Federationist,* 1894, I, 205, contains the list of labor candidates.

28. Lloyd to Samuel Gompers, Aug. 14, 1894, Lloyd Papers, WHS.

29. A. M. McLean to Edwin Atwood, June 19, 1890, Atwood Papers, Oliver T. Erickson to Donnelly, Jan. 25, 1892, Donnelly Papers, and H. P. Bjorge to Charles Brandborg, Apr. 2, 1891, Brandborg Papers, all in MHS.

30. *Representative* (St. Paul, Minn.), Nov. 21, 1894, Feb. 20, 1895, MHS.

31. Robert Sturgeon to Solomon Comstock, July 21, 1891, Comstock Papers, MHS.

CHAPTER FOUR

Philosophic Digression

1. See above, pp. 25-27; Karl Marx, *Economic and Philosophic Manuscripts of 1844* (Moscow, 1956), pp. 72-73, 70, 75, 77.

2. See above, pp. 33-35; Karl Marx, *Capital* (Modern Library, New York, n.d.), I, 806, 785-786, 786.

3. See above, pp. 18-20, 15, 13, 31; Karl Marx, *German Ideology* (New York, 1947), p. 39; Marx, *Capital,* I, 188; Marx, *German Ideology,* p. 22.

4. See above, pp. 40, 21; Karl Marx, *Selected Essays* (London, 1926), pp. 11-12.

5. See above, pp. 17, 27-29; Marx, *Capital,* I, 836, 673, 189, III,

568. The last citation is quoted as part of an extremely interesting analysis in Paul M. Sweezy, *The Theory of Capitalist Development* (London, 1942), p. 177.

6. *Ibid.*, p. 178.

7. See above, pp. 29–31; Marx, *Capital*, I, 701, 691–692, 693; Karl Marx and Frederick Engels, *Manifesto of the Communist Party*, in their *Selected Works* (Moscow, 1955), I, 37; Marx, *Capital*, I, 649, 689.

8. See above, pp. 37, 28; Karl Marx, *A Contribution to the Critique of Political Economy*, in *Selected Works*, I, 363.

9. George K. Holmes, "The Concentration of Wealth," *Political Science Quarterly*, 8:593 (December 1893). See *Alliance* (Lincoln, Neb.), Nov. 9, 1889, NHS, for the analysis of another statistical study on wealth concentration.

10. *Platte County Argus* (Columbus, Neb.), Oct. 15, 22, 1896, NHS.

11. *Saunders County New Era* (Wahoo, Neb.), Mar. 4, May 14, 1896, and *Custer County Beacon* (Broken Bow, Neb.), Sept. 12, 1895, both in NHS.

12. Blanton Duncan to Donnelly, Mar. 26, Apr. 3, 1894, Donnelly Papers, MHS.

13. *Advocate* (Topeka, Kan.), Mar. 7, 1894, KSHS; Eugene V. Debs to Lloyd, July 24, 1894, and Thomas V. Cator to Lloyd, Dec. 3, 1894, both in Lloyd Papers, WHS.

14. *Alliance* (Lincoln, Neb.), Nov. 16, 1889, and *Farmers' Alliance* (Lincoln, Neb.), June 21, 1890, both in NHS.

15. *Farmers' Alliance* (Lincoln, Neb.), Mar. 10, 1892, *Saunders County New Era* (Wahoo, Neb.), Jan. 16, Aug. 7, 1896, and *Polk County Independent* (Osceola, Neb.), Feb. 27, 1896, all in NHS; M. W. Colburn to Lewelling, May 16, 1892, Lewelling Papers, KSHS.

16. S. S. King, *Bond-Holders and Bread-Winners* (Kansas City, 1892), pp. 62–63, in *People's Party Pamphlets*, IV, KSHS.

17. J. Keir Hardie to Lloyd, Aug. 22, 1890, and Sidney Webb to Lloyd, June 4, 1890, both in Lloyd Papers, WHS.

18. Frederick Engels to Lloyd, May 27, 1893, Lloyd Papers, WHS. To my knowledge this letter has not appeared before; it is not contained in Karl Marx and Frederick Engels, *Letters to Americans, 1848–1895* (New York, 1953).

CHAPTER FIVE

Sectarian Politics: The Socialist Labor Party Attack on Populism

1. Engels to F. A. Sorge, May 12, 1894, quoted in Marx and Engels, *Letters to Americans,* p. 263.

2. Report of National Executive Committee, Socialist Labor Party, July 4, 1896, S.L.P. Papers, WHS.

3. G. A. Hoehn, July [n.d. but probably at national convention], 1896, S.L.P. Papers, WHS.

4. Paul Ehrmann to Lloyd, July 3, 1896, Lloyd Papers, WHS.

5. *The People* (New York), Dec. 17, 1893, Tamiment Library, New York.

6. A. Urison to [?], Mar. 22, 1896, De Leon Papers, and W. J. Guymon to J. Wilson Becker, June 19, 1896, S.L.P. Papers, both in WHS.

7. J. Wilson Becker to Henry Kuhn, June 17, 27, 1896, S.L.P. Papers, WHS.

8. Charles B. Kirkbride to Charles H. Matchett, Aug. 27, 1896, De Leon Papers, M. W. Wilkins to Kuhn, Sept. 8, 1896, S.L.P. Papers, and Fred Fellermann to De Leon, Jan. 10, 1896, De Leon Papers, all in WHS.

9. George B. Leonard to De Leon, Jan. 27, 1896, De Leon Papers, WHS.

10. *Advocate* (Topeka, Kan.), Nov. 22, 1893, KSHS.

11. *Ibid.*, Feb. 14, Nov. 14, 1894.

12. *Custer County Beacon* (Broken Bow, Neb.), Oct. 17, 1889, NHS.

13. H. H. Haaff to editor, *Farmers' Alliance* (Lincoln, Neb.), June 7, 1890, and *Alliance-Independent* (Lincoln, Neb.), May 25, 1893, both in NHS.

14. Lloyd to George A. Gates, May 23, 1895, Lloyd Papers, WHS.

15. Lloyd to W. G. Eggleston, Dec. 29, 1890, Lloyd Papers, WHS. I am not discussing here Lloyd's total work; his *Wealth Against Commonwealth,* for example, is the subject of an important essay in Destler.

16. Willis J. Abbot to Lloyd, Aug. 13, 1894, and Debs to Lloyd, Aug. 15, 1894, Lloyd Papers, WHS. See *Times* (Chicago), Nov. 8, 1894, for a vote tabulation. Running in his silk stocking Winnetka district, Lloyd received only 5,891 votes out of over 36,000 ballots cast.

17. Darrow to Lloyd, Nov. 22, 1894, and Lloyd to Darrow,

Nov. 23, 1894, Lloyd Papers, WHS. The exchange once again underscored Lloyd's belief that increasing oppression would stimulate the growth of radicalism. Darrow, with the union convictions in mind, lamented: "The People are dead. Can any thing be done to resurrect them before liberty is dead. I am very much discouraged at the prospect." Lloyd, stating that he expected the convictions, reached a very different conclusion: "Where the plutes are wrong is in their folly of supposing that they can cure this evil *by force*." He concluded, "It is only by aggressions of the enemy that the people can be united. Events must be our leaders, and we will have them. I am not discouraged. The radicalism of the fanatics of wealth fills me with hope."

18. Frank W. Elliott to Henry Kuhn, Sept. 1, 1896, S.L.P. Papers, WHS.

19. E. T. Tucker to Kuhn, Sept. 5, 18, 1896, and Frank O'Neil to National Executive Committee, Oct. 17, 1896, both in S.L.P. Papers, WHS.

20. Thomas J. Morgan to Lloyd, July 6, 1896, Lloyd Papers, WHS. See Destler, chaps. viii and xi, esp. pp. 171–174, 243–245, for the Illinois situation.

21. Joseph B. Keim to New Jersey state central committee, Socialist Labor Party, Aug. 25, 1896, De Leon Papers, WHS.

CHAPTER SIX

Fusion: The Last Assertion of Populist Radicalism

1. Henry D. Lloyd, "The Populists at St. Louis," *Review of Reviews*, 14:299, 301–303 (September 1896).

2. *Advocate* (Topeka, Kan.), Nov. 22, Dec. 20, 1893, Jan. 3, 1894, KSHS.

3. *Ibid.*, Mar. 13, 1895.

4. *Ibid.*, June 10, 17, 1896.

5. *Ibid.*, July 15, 29, Aug. 5, 1896.

6. *Ibid.*, Oct. 21, 1896.

7. *Ibid.*, Nov. 11, 1896.

8. *Alliance-Independent* (Lincoln, Neb.), Jan. 18, 1894, *Wealth Makers* (Lincoln, Neb.), Jan. 24, 31, 1895, and John Stebbins to editor, *Wealth Makers*, Jan. 31, 1895, all in NHS.

9. *Wealth Makers* (Lincoln, Neb.), Feb. 14, Apr. 25, 1895, NHS.

10. F. Houchin and H. E. Dawes to editor, *ibid.*, May 1, 1895.

11. *Nebraska Independent* (Lincoln, Neb.), Apr. 30, 1896,

NHS; Thad Williams, J. A. Baird, H. Greathouse, J. B. Romine, Theo. Mahn, and W. L. Stark, to editor, *ibid.*, July 16, 1896.

12. *Ibid.*, July 30, Aug. 6, 13, Oct. 8, 1896.

13. *Custer County Beacon* (Broken Bow, Neb.), Mar. 24, 1892, Nov. 21, 28, Dec. 12, 26, 1895, NHS.

14. *Ibid.*, Jan. 2, 1896; A. B. Hartley to editor, *ibid.*, Jan. 16, 1896; *ibid.*, Jan. 16, 1896.

15. James Holland to editor, *ibid.*, Mar. 12, 1896.

16. *Ibid.*, Apr. 29, May 14, 1896.

17. *Saunders County New Era* (Wahoo, Neb.), Feb. 13, 1896, NHS.

18. James B. Weaver to William Jennings Bryan, Sept. 1, Nov. 9, 1894, Bryan Papers, LC.

19. Weaver to Donnelly, Jan. 13, 1895, Donnelly Papers, MHS.

20. Weaver to Donnelly, Mar. 20, 23, 1895, Donnelly Papers, MHS.

21. Weaver to Bryan, Dec. 31, 1895, May 29, 1896, Bryan Papers, L.C.

22. Davis Waite to Donnelly, Apr. 22, Aug. 22, 1895, Donnelly Papers, MHS; J. L. Perkins to Luhman Weller, May 13, 1896, Weller Papers, WHS.

23. *World Herald* (Omaha, Neb.), Nov. 11, 1894, in Bryan Scrapbook, II, NHS. See Bryan to Donnelly, Nov. 13, 1895, Donnelly Papers, MHS, for the possibility that he was more radical than his editorials would seem to indicate: "I cannot say as much editorially as I would like to because I am now doing what I can to get the silver democrats to capture the national convention."

24. Bryan to Horace Boies, May 3, 1892, copy in Bryan Papers, LC.

25. Bryan to W. S. Bissel, Oct. 24, 1893, Bryan Papers, LC.

26. Donnelly to Weaver, Jan. 18, 1895, Donnelly Papers, MHS.

27. J. Sterling Morton to R. W. Furnas, June 27, 1896, Morton to William T. Baker, June 27, 1896, and Morton to Euclid Martin, June 27, 1896, Morton Papers, NHS.

28. Seth W. Cobb to Morton, July 6, 1896, and W. W. Cox to Morton, July 17, 1896, Morton Papers, NHS.

29. Charles W. Dabney to Morton, Aug. 15, 1896, Morton to W. L. Wilson, Oct. 18, 1896, and Morton to Joy Morton, Oct. 19, 24, 1896, Morton Papers, NHS.

30. Morton to Joy Morton, Oct. 29, 1896, Morton to Mark Morton, Oct. 29, 1896, Morton to George L. Miller, Oct. 30, 1896, and Morton to J. R. Buchanan, Nov. 10, 1896, Morton Papers, NHS.
31. Waite to Donnelly, Feb. 4, 1894, Donnelly Papers, MHS; Waite to Lewelling, July 12, 1894, Lewelling Papers, KSHS.
32. Waite to Donnelly, Dec. 11, 1894, Donnelly Papers, MHS; Waite to Bryan, Nov. 26, 1895, Bryan Papers, LC.
33. *Democrat* (St. Louis), July 21, 1896, in Donnelly Scrapbooks, C, MHS.
34. Blanton Duncan to editor, Apr. 3, 1895, A. S. Stephens to editor, Apr. 10, 1895, and A. J. McPhee to editor, Apr. 25, 1895, all in *Representative* (St. Paul), MHS.
35. *Advocate* (Topeka, Kan.), Jan. 30, Mar. 27, 1895, KSHS; *Polk County Independent* (Osceola, Neb.), May 14, 1896, NHS.
36. T. L. Nugent to editor, *Custer County Beacon* (Broken Bow, Neb.), Sept. 26, 1895, NHS.
37. W. H. Mellen to editor, *Phelps County Weekly Progress* (Holdredge, Neb.), July 3, 1896, NHS.
38. George F. Washburn to Donnelly, Feb. 13, 1895, Donnelly Papers, MHS; *Custer County Beacon* (Broken Bow, Neb.), May 28, 1896, NHS.
39. Lloyd to J. F. Paulsen, Dec. 10, 1893, and Lloyd to C. A. Powers, Dec. 16, 1894, Lloyd Papers, WHS.
40. George H. Gibson to Lloyd, Dec. 10, 1894, Henry R. Legate to Lloyd, Dec. 10, 1894, and Phoebe W. Couzins to Lloyd, Dec. 30, 1894, Lloyd Papers, WHS.
41. Henry R. Legate to Lloyd, May 13, June 7, 1896, and A. B. Adair to Lloyd, May 30, 1896, Lloyd Papers, WHS.
42. Lloyd to R. I. Grimes, July 10, 1896, Lloyd Papers, WHS.
43. Bayard Holmes to Lloyd, July 11, 1896, and Lloyd to Holmes, July 13, 1896, Lloyd Papers, WHS. In the first, Holmes closed with an interesting portrayal of Bryan: "He is . . . a most devoted and even religious man and I believe he has no ambition except to serve his country. He seems to be imbued with the spirit of a martyr and with a wisdom which baffles commercial antagonism."
44. Sylvester Baxter to Lloyd, Aug. 1, 1896, and Lloyd to James H. Ferriss, Aug. 6, 1896, Lloyd Papers, WHS.
45. Lloyd to A. B. Adair, Oct. 10, 1896, Lloyd Papers, WHS. See Caro Lloyd, *Henry Demarest Lloyd* (New York, 1912), I, 265, for Lloyd's final stand in the election.

INDEX

DATE DUE

MAR 1 3 '64			
NOV 1 ~ 6			
NOV 1 6 '64			
MAR 2 4 '65			
MAY 1 3 '65			
MAY 1 4 '65			
MAR 1 5 67			
APR 9 '68			
DE~ ~ '~			
GAYLORD			PRINTED IN U.S.A.